OMPANY ISLANDS

Torres Strait

Cape York

Cape Arnhem

Gulf of Carpenteria

PELLEW ISLANDS

WELLESLEY ISLANDS

THE GREAT BARRIER REEFS

Cumberland Islands

WRECK ISLAND

Northumberland Islands

Hervey Bay

L I A

Brisbane

Moreton Bay

PORT LINCOLN

Mount Lofty

Adelaide

ENCOUNTER BAY

Sydney (Port Jackson)
Botany Bay

GULF

KANGAROO ISLAND

Melbourne

TWO FOLD BAY

NCENT

PORT PHILIP

Western Port

BASS'S STRAIT

King Island

Flinders' Island

CAPE GRIM

Tasmania (Van Diemen's Land)

Hobart

STORM BAY

The

Fever of Discovery

That genuine spirit of discovery
which contemns all danger and
inconveniences with its gratification

Matthew Flinders
A Voyage to Terra Australis

THE

FEVER OF DISCOVERY

The story of
Matthew Flinders

who gave Australia her name

Marion Body

New European Publications

Published in the United Kingdom in 2006 by

New European Publications Limited
14-16 Carroun Road
London SW8 1JT, England

British Library Cataloguing in Publication Data

ISBN 1-872410-45-6

Typesetting by KAD

Printed and bound in Great Britain by Antony Rowe, Chippenham, Wiltshire.

Contents

Toussaint Antoine De Chazal De Chamerel,
Mauritius, 1770-1822.

Portrait of Captain Matthew Flinders, RN, 1774-1814.
1806-7, Mauritius.

Oil on canvas
64.5 x 50.0 cms.

Gift of David Roche in memory of his father, J D K
Roche; and the South Australian Government 2000.

Art Gallery of South Australia, Adelaide.

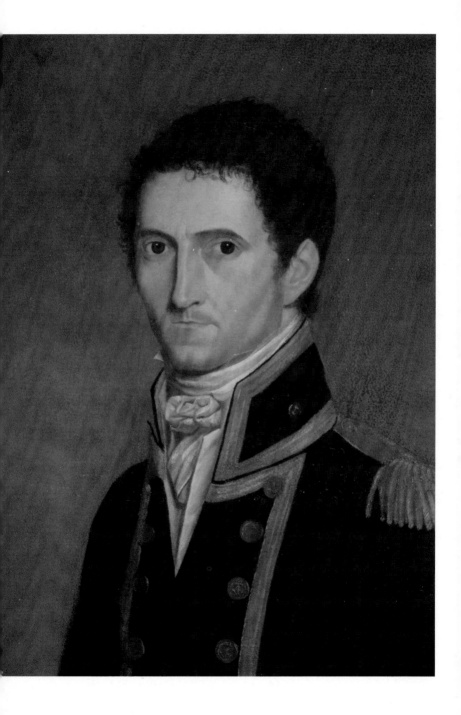

Acknowledgements

The Fever of Discovery is the result of several years of research originally made for personal interest. Since it was suggested that I should write a book, I have attempted to distil that research to tell the story of the life and achievements of Matthew Flinders.

It would not have been written without the help of members of the Flinders' family. Above all I would like to remember Ann Flinders Petrie, who before she died in 1989 told me about the life of her great grandfather, lending or giving me copies of some of his writings. It was she who inspired my interest and to whom this book is dedicated.

My thanks are given to Lisette Flinders Petrie, Ann's niece, who has given permission to quote from personal letters and papers and to use her copy of the miniature of Matthew Flinders; Witgar Hitchcock and Ann Cox, both descendants of Matthew's sister and Keith Flinders, a descendant of Matthew's great-great-grandfather.

The State Library of New South Wales, Sydney has given permission to quote from Matthew Flinders' journals of the *Investigator* 1801-1803 and from his private journal 1803-1814; they have also allowed quotations from Samuel Smith's diary.

Permission has been given by the National Library of Australia, Canberra to reproduce the sketch made by William Westall on Kangaroo Island, and his drawing of Government House, Sydney.

The Art Gallery of South Australia, Adelaide has permitted the use of Matthew Flinders' portrait by Toussaint Antoine de Chazal de Chamerel.

Flinders University, Adelaide has allowed the reproduction of a letter written by Matthew Flinders and the drawing by Ann Flinders, both now in the Flinders Collection. I am especially grateful to Sheryl Chandler for her help and enthusiasm, to Dr Gillian Dooley and to Dr Peter Monteath who let me use a copy of his edited version of Samuel Smith's diary, *Sailing with Flinders*.

The National Maritime Museum, Greenwich allowed me to read and quote from the Library's original edition of *A Voyage to Terra Australis*; to read Matthew Flinders' personal papers which are on loan by the Flinders family, including the story of *Trim* and *The Cruize of the Tom Thumb*; joint permission has been given to quote. They have also allowed a drawing to be made from a photograph of Flinders' birthplace. My thanks are given to Dr Nigel Rigby for his help and advice.

Permission has been received from the United Kingdom Hydrographic Office, to reproduce Matthew Flinders' original map of Australia and to use information about charting the western coast.

Permission to reproduce Ferdinand Bauer's drawing has been given by the Natural History Museum, London.

The Dean and Chapter of Lincoln Cathedral gave permission for a photograph to be taken of the model of the *Investigator* which hangs in the Seamen's Chapel, and to reproduce it. Lincolnshire Archives and Robert and Ursula Perry have given permission to use short extracts from the diary of Matthew Flinders' father.

Those in Lincolnshire who have given me information

include the Reverend Canon Rex Davis, Sue Ridley and Ken Hinton, all of the Britain-Australia Society (Lincolnshire Branch); John Cammack, the Boston Historical Society; Adrian Hallett, former Headmaster of The Cowley School, Donington; Sheila Robson; Chantal Armstrong; Ruby Hunt.

There are a number of people in Australia to whom I am grateful for their help on my visits and in particular Paul Brunton, State Library of New South Wales, the Hon. Neil Lucas, PRM, MLC, Dick and Yvonne Austen, and Pauline Glenie.

There are many others to whom I must express thanks and they include Captain Michael Barrow, CVO. DSO. RN., for information about the Flinders' Bar, Captain Hugh Owen, RN, and Lieutenant Commander Peter Ashley, RN.

Also to Dr David Shepherd, University of Reading for his introduction to Dr Jairaj Ramkisson, Ministry of Agriculture, Mauritius; Robin Brodhurst and Ian Busby, Pangbourne College; Edward Holloway; Rachel Rowe, Royal Commonwealth Society; James Holloway, National Gallery of Scotland.

My thanks go to John Coleman, Maurice Temple-Smith, Helen Carroll, Lloyd Allen, Janet Callender; to Ken and Andrea Downing for their great patience with typesetting this book; and also Margaret Clarke and Sarah Scott-Johnson for their secretarial work.

My family deserve my thanks, particularly my daughter, Jane, for her interest and her illustration, and my husband, Richard, for all his patience and encouragement whilst I have been seized with the fever of research.

Marion Body

To the happy memory of
Ann Flinders Petrie

Introduction

In October 1800 Napoleon sent out to the southern hemisphere two expensively equipped ships to gain scientific knowledge of the lands then known as New Holland and New South Wales and to carry out surveys of the coasts, with particular interest in the southern coast. If it had not been for Matthew Flinders, the history of the land he named Australia might have been different.

Dutch, Spanish, Portuguese, French and Chinese navigators had sighted various parts of the coasts and James Cook, having landed at Botany Bay had sailed up the eastern coast, naming the whole stretch New South Wales, which then led to the founding of a British colony at Sydney Cove in 1788. The southern coast, however, had never been sighted and therefore the French were anxious to be the first to claim original discovery, which would enable them to claim possession.

Napoleon himself and many learned men in France were interested in pure scientific research but there was an underlying desire to be the first to survey this coastline. Furthermore, the French had possessions and considerable influence in the area of the Indian Ocean and some saw the possible colonisation of this new land as a threat to their power. In a report written by a member of the French expedition it is recommended that Sydney should be destroyed, an operation that might have been feasible if Napoleon had founded a settlement on the southern coast.

In September 1800 Matthew Flinders, then aged 27, volunteered to return to New South Wales, where he had served for six years in the Navy. During that time he had, with George Bass, discovered the Bass Strait and was the first to sail round the whole coast of Tasmania.

He was given command of a small ship, once used as a collier and then adapted for convoy duties in the English Channel. She leaked badly and many of her inner timbers were later found to be rotten. Accompanied by a small team of botanists and artists Flinders sailed from England in July 1801 to discover and chart accurately the southern coast, meeting the French expedition coming from the opposite direction having achieved only 150 miles of original discovery.

Matthew Flinders then went on to be the first to circumnavigate the continent and to prove it was one great landmass, not divided into two islands as had been thought previously. His charts were so accurate that many were in use for about 140 years and some of his instructions are followed to this day. In the 1960's a new survey was made of the large area south of Borneo and it included part of the northern coast of Australia. Sophisticated instruments were used and aerial photographs taken, but when the transparencies were laid over Flinders' charts, which had been made with far simpler instruments, they were found to fit exactly with only one or two very minor exceptions. This is the more remarkable when it is considered that Flinders, unlike Cook, was entirely self-taught.

His work on the effect on the compass of the magnetism caused by iron in ships was a major contribution to the safety of navigation and resulted in the adoption of the Flinders Bar, still carried on ships today.

The Dutch, the Portuguese and the Spaniards had traded in the East Indies since about 1540 and had known there was land to the south which was called Terra Australis, Terra Australis Incognita or The Great South Land. In

1605 a Spanish expedition coming from Peru to find the land which their leader, de Quiros, called Australia del Espirito Santo may have sighted the north eastern coast, but it was de Torres, commanding the accompanying ship which got separated in a storm, who certainly sighted what we now call Cape York. In 1642 the Dutchman, Abel Tasman, set off from Batavia to Mauritius from where he steered south and eastwards arriving at what he named Antony van Diemen's Land, in honour of the Governor of Batavia, but the island we know as Tasmania, and in 1644 he was also to explore the Gulf of Carpentaria. The Dutch named the western part of the new land New Holland, but the southern and eastern coasts remained the great unknown until James Cook landed at Botany Bay in April 1770 and further attempts were made by both French and English navigators in the following years.

Flinders having suggested that the whole continent should be called Australia, used the name frequently and in 1806 wrote to the President of the Royal Society, Sir Joseph Banks "about my discoveries in Australia" and he referred to the native people as Australians. It was he who drew the first map of Australia and it is a lasting memorial to his discoveries and his dedication.

A man of considerable intellect and a great navigator and mathematician, Flinders was born at a time when not only were the arts flourishing, but when there were great advances in scientific knowledge and in exploration overseas. He was fired with enthusiasm by the voyages of James Cook whose nautical grandson he felt himself to be, and seemingly he became gripped with a fever to make a significant contribution to the discoveries of the age. Not only have many of Flinders' journals and reports survived, but also his letters, both official ones and those written to his wife.

Some years ago the District Council, meeting in Spalding a few miles from his birthplace, were debating whether or not to buy a handsome bronze bust of Flinders that was for sale. During the discussion a councillor remarked "Who is this geezer Matthew Flinders?" — which sadly sums up the fact that although honoured in Australia, Flinders' name is little known in England, except in his native village of Donington in Lincolnshire, where his memory is certainly kept green. His story is a riveting saga of an unsung hero. Had he been a Yorkshireman and not a modest Yellowbelly, as true Lincolnshire men are called, it is one that would have been told at every mother's knee.

It is hoped that this book will interest Australians and will help to spread interest in England in the story of the triumph, tragedy and romance of the life of Matthew Flinders.

Son of Lincolnshire

The forebears of Matthew Flinders are believed to have come from Flanders and to have settled at Ruddington in Nottinghamshire about 1550, where they became stocking makers. It is thought that one of them moved to Lincolnshire and worked with Cornelius Vermuyden who began the drainage of the Fens in 1621. The family became graziers, until Matthew's grandfather, John Flinders, practised medicine in Spalding, to be followed by his son, Matthew, who was a surgeon in Donington when his eldest son, Matthew, was born there on 16th March 1774.

Although a main road now runs nearby and new houses have been built over the years, the shape of the centre of the village would be recognisable to him, but his own home was pulled down in 1908. It is possible to imagine him running across the green to school, The Cowley Free School, founded by Thomas Cowley in 1719. The school was on two floors — one floor for boys, the other for girls — and it had a bell tower. When few people had clocks this must have been meant to ensure that pupils were not late for school. The building was replaced in 1812. That attractive building still stands, but is backed by modern ones for its 570 pupils and the assembly room is built on the site of Matthew's school room.

He would have walked more circumspectly with his parents to Donington Parish Church, Saint Mary and the Holy Rood, where he had been baptised. Parts of this church date from the 13th century and there is now a window dedicated to his memory and to the memories of Sir Joseph Banks and George Bass, three Lincolnshire men who did much to add to our knowledge of the largely undiscovered land in the southern seas.

Matthew's mother, Susanah (née Ward) died when he was nine years old, leaving five children; his father then married Elizabeth Weekes. They brought up the children strictly, as was the usual custom of the time, but friends and relatives came to stay, among them the Franklin children, whose mother Hannah Weekes was sister to Elizabeth and married to Willingham Franklin of Spilsby. Their son, John Franklin, was to sail with Matthew, become Governor of Van Diemen's Land and later to lose his life when exploring the Arctic.

It is likely that visits were exchanged with George Bass: although not known for certain, Matthew's great-grand-daughter, Ann Flinders Petrie thought that they did. They were distant cousins, both being great-grandsons of John Flinders whose third daughter married into the Bass family. George was born at Aswarby but his parents moved to Boston and it is probable that he attended the Grammar School. His father is believed to have been on friendly terms with Matthew's father.

If they did meet they would have known the Market Place in Boston and many of the ancient narrow lanes in the centre of the town, such as Craythorn Lane, Pump Lane and Wormgate. They would recognise the Guildhall, Pescod Hall, Church Key House, and some early Georgian houses. Just as we do today they would have marvelled at St. Botolph's church, always known as The Stump, that huge majestic building which is the largest parish church in England, whose tower of 272 feet dominates the town and can be seen for miles across the Fens. The boys may have looked at the books in the church's ancient library which still exists in a room above the south door, and perhaps taken a ghoulish delight in the illustrations of Foxe's *Book of Martyrs*, whose author was born in a house at the corner of the Market Place and Fish Hill. They might have enjoyed the great sheep fairs and watched the fishing boats and above all the larger merchant ships sailing in.

In Donington there was a rope walk, and they would have seen the ropes being made for the rigging of ships, the hemp for which grew in the fields around the town. Flocks of geese were kept on the marshes, a by-product being the wing feathers used for quill pens. Matthew became a prolific writer and one cannot begin to guess the number of quills he must have used in his lifetime. Matthew spent much time on the marshes and watching the wildfowl: a story is told of him being lost for hours and being found with his pocket full of stones which he was using as markers in trying to find the sources of small streams. He is likely to have visited Spalding where his uncle was a surgeon, and houses he knew such as Ascoughe Hall with its great yew hedges and many of the early Georgian houses still stand today.

At the age of twelve Matthew was sent as a boarder to Horbling Grammar School, a small establishment run by the Reverend John Shinglar and where teaching took place in a room in the church. Seeing he had a pupil who had great potential Mr Shinglar helped him to develop his neat, elegant handwriting and his happy turn of phrase. He allowed Matthew to study mathematics widely and to read books outside the rigid school curriculum. It was at Horbling that Matthew first read *Robinson Crusoe*, a book which fired his imagination, and a copy of which he kept with him all his life. Some thirty years later he wrote that he had been induced to go to sea against the wishes of friends from reading *Robinson Crusoe*, and a week or so before his death he ordered a new copy.

Matthew, while still at Horbling, wrote to his cousin, John Flinders, then serving in the Navy as a Sub-Lieutenant, to ask his advice. He received a discouraging reply as John was disillusioned by his own slow progress and advised him that without friends of influence it was difficult to get promotion. Nevertheless he added that if he was determined, then he should study navigation and trigonometry. Acting on this advice, Matthew spent the next year in private study of those subjects, much to the surprise of Mr. Lound the headmaster of the Cowley School. His father, realising that he had inherited a scientific brain, hoped his son would follow him in his surgeon's practice and tried to dissuade him from a life at sea with its dangers and hardships, sending him to Lincoln for instruction in medicine. With an adventurous spirit, further fuelled by hearing of the great voyages of discovery of Captain James Cook, Matthew remained determined: in face of the determination that was to carry him through his life, his father eventually agreed.

The great chance came in an unlikely way, through his cousin, Henrietta Flinders. She was the governess to the family of Captain T.S. Pasley, who was commanding *HMS Scipio*. He invited young Flinders to visit him and it has always been believed that, impressed with his ability and enthusiasm, he found him a place on the training ship *Alert*, moored in the Medway. According to new research carried out by Lieutenant Commander Peter Ashley it seems that Matthew's cousin John Flinders, serving in *HMS Europa* in the West Indies, was a friend of Robert Laurie serving in the sloop *Alert*, also in the West Indies. He asked Laurie to get Matthew's name on the ship's book as a Lieutenant's

Servant, which he did in October 1789. Although it seems a doubtful arrangement, others did the same for the reason that a young man intended for the upper deck had to serve six years before being considered for promotion to lieutenant. Therefore, if his name appeared on a ship's muster it cut down the time before he was eligible. Possibly a payment was made, but as young Matthew had no money, and it is most unlikely that his father would have helped him, it is difficult to know how he could have done it himself. Nevertheless his name is on the ship's muster, now in the Public Record Office at Kew, until August 1790, which was three months after Captain Pasley took him aboard *HMS Scipio*, and it can only be guessed that it was he who may have thus used his influence.

From his father's diary we know that Matthew was still at home until May 1790, when he recorded:

> Went with Matthew to Spalding to take coach for London, thence to Rochester to Command. Pasley's to embark in the Scipio 64 guns. It has long been his choice, not mine. Henny got him in this situation, pray God it may be to his advantage. I have letters of his arrival and Content. I suppose he will be in the capacity of Midshipman, the stipend of which is but bare subsistence. I shall heavily miss him.

Arrived on board *HMS Scipio* he would have learned naval routine and the basic rules of seamanship and it would also have been a test as to whether he would stand up to harsh conditions of life at sea. Today on the rare occasions that we see a ship in full sail, such as when the replica of the *Endeavour* sailed into Boston, we marvel at its beauty, but life aboard was tough indeed with cramped quarters, poor food, shortages of water and a complement of rats. His childhood home was probably fairly comfortable by the standards of the day but the food would have been simple, all water and fuel carried into the house and so used sparingly. Houses and school rooms were cold when the north and east winds blew in from the North Sea across the great flat fenlands of Lincolnshire, so he would have adapted quickly to the conditions aboard ship. Pasley was shortly afterwards given command of the *Bellepheron* and he took Matthew with him. Equipped with 74 guns, the *Bellepheron* was one of the great ships of the line which was to be engaged in a number of notable actions, including Trafalgar, and was to take Napoleon to exile in St Helena. Her name stemmed from Greek mythology, but she was affectionately known among the seamen as the *Billy Ruffian*.

In May 1791 he transferred as a midshipman to *HMS Providence* under the command of Captain William Bligh, then fitting out for his second Breadfruit Voyage. Everyone knows the story of the mutiny in the *Bounty*, but much of the truth is hidden or forgotten. As ever, the conditions were harsh and Bligh was strict, but the crew having spent several months in Tahiti enjoying comparative luxury whilst the loading of the breadfruit plants took place, to say nothing of the charms of the beautiful women, were in no mood to face the hardships of the long, hot voyage to the West Indies. So having rebelled, they put Bligh and a few others in a small open boat, and by a tremendous feat of navigation, he reached Timor and finally got back to England. He was later to become Governor General of New South Wales.

Flinders was seventeen when Bligh in command of the *Providence* sailed in 1791 and was away until August 1793. Three months was spent in Tahiti loading breadfruit and other plants to take to the Caribbean, followed by four months in Jamaica, where the ship was needed to protect the area from the French. The officers and crew had been

very carefully picked this time and Flinders helped with
the care of the time-keepers — an extremely important
task from which longitude and the position of the ship
could be calculated more accurately by the use of the sea
going clocks invented by John Harrison. These were to
revolutionise the measurement of longitude and had only
been adopted after a great deal of opposition from the
Board of Longitude and the Astronomer Royal, Sir Nevil
Maskelyne.

Flinders gained much from this voyage learning from
Bligh how men on long voyages could be kept in reasonable
health, free from scurvy, which was something that Bligh
had learnt when he had served as Master of the *Resolution*
under Captain Cook. On the Breadfruit Voyage water
had to be rationed very severely because the plants being
carried had to have priority and seamen sometimes licked
the leaves in order to get extra drops of moisture in the
heat. Flinders learnt how to approach an unknown coast,
to understand the day to day routine, making up the ship's
logbook and making one of his own for good measure,
written with the enthusiasm of a young man, and adding a
number of sketches. On one page he gives an account of
the "treatment of the ship's company with respect to the
provisions" giving details of the daily rations, something
which would be of great value when he had the charge of
his own crew. He learnt to deal with native people, either
those who were friendly or those who attacked in canoes
off the coast of New Guinea.

On the outward voyage they sailed by way of South
Africa and along the southern coast of Tasmania where
on landing at Adventure Bay Flinders made a sketch. On
the return voyage they were under orders to find a new
passage through the Torres Strait, an experience which was
invaluable to Flinders later on.

Although conditions were harsh, Bligh did allow some relaxation and Flinders wrote an account of the ceremony of crossing the Equator. He described how after dinner "the Boatswain piped All Hands to Mischief" and those who had crossed the line before erected a triangular gallows attached to which there was an iron hoop, filed sharp at one edge, and prepared a pair of buckets. The first contained every kind of filth they could collect, into which would be dipped any man who refused to give any liquor: the second bucket held oatmeal and water and which no-one was allowed to escape. A large tub of sea water and plenty of buckets completed the scene.

The non-equatorians, as Flinders called them, were sent below and the hatchways covered, with a sentry placed by each. A voice was heard hailing the ship and another calling that the most noble Neptune and his retinue would be welcome aboard. Presently two seamen "who styled themselves constables, came down with their faces blacked, deputed by Neptune to bring up Mr Nichols who was first on the list. They fixed a handkerchief over his eyes and led him up the other hatchway, walking on each side of him with tridents or broomsticks in their hands as marks of their authority".

A great deal of swashing of water and laughter was heard, and each man in turn was fetched. "They blinded me and made me sit down. Oh these gallows thinks I, however they began to tell me that Neptune was come on board, they hoped I would not let him go without something to drink and asked how much I proposed to give him…. How much do you want? One answers the Gentleman won't think much of a gallon. No says another, half will do. The Captain says why he must give you a bottle, the same as the rest. Yes, says Neptune a bottle will do."

Flinders' face was daubed with the oatmeal mixture and scraped with the razor before Neptune ordered a wash. "My seat went from under me. I fell backward in the water. Sluice comes half a dozen buckets over me". The blindfold being taken off, he found himself in a large tub of water, and everybody with buckets heaving water at him and on his left the Gunner's Mate disguised as Neptune, and two seamen as his wife and the barber, painted black with black swabs for tails. Flinders records that "without any remorse of conscience I got in with the rest and sluiced away at the next poor devil that came". Some of those who had crossed the line before got up into the tops to avoid getting wet, but were quickly followed up and sluiced. A water war broke out which was only given up by the Captain "expressing a desire that it should". Everyone went below, put on clean clothes and the Captain gave each man a dram.

In later life Flinders wrote that he would not have wished to serve again under the stern leadership of Bligh, but he acknowledged that the experience was invaluable to him and he made it clear that he felt an affinity with Captain Cook through Captain Bligh.

Flinders was brought up on the Fens with their wide skies and great sunsets, but those skies are often grey and English colours are soft. Seeing the brilliant colours of tropical countries, the sunshine and the sparkling seas gave him a great sense of excitement and adventure which strengthened his resolve to return there if he could. Although they did not have any personal regard for each other, Bligh gave a good report of him, and one month after his return Flinders rejoined the *Bellepheron* as aide-de-camp to Thomas Pasley, now Rear Admiral.

In the spring of 1794 intelligence was received that the

French, being desperately short of food, had bought American grain which was being shipped to France in 117 ships and that the French Fleet would meet them off Cape Finistère to escort them to Brest. The British Grand Fleet set sail to find such thick fog that it was difficult to see anything let alone find the French Fleet. Encountering a Dutch ship they were told that the French were 200 miles to the south. At two in the morning on the 1st June the fog cleared and the French were seen at dawn. The battle known to history as the Glorious First of June took place leaving the French Fleet seriously defeated, although it has to be said that the convoy carrying the food did reach Brest.

During the battle the *Bellepheron* was attacked on both sides by enemy ships, her main sail was badly damaged and three top masts were shot away. Flinders behaved with courage and enthusiasm and when men at the guns were ordered to attempt to clear the entangled sails he fired without orders the guns on the quarter deck which were loaded and primed. Pasley reprimanded him, shaking him by the collar, when he replied coolly that the opportunity would have been missed if he had not done so. He survived the battle unscathed but Admiral Pasley was badly wounded and lost a leg. Flinders instantly wrote an account of the battle which is now in possession of the National Maritime Museum at Greenwich.

2

To Terra Australis

On returning to England, Flinders was awarded a period of leave in Lincolnshire where he received a hero's welcome. He always tried to keep in touch with home: in writing to the Franklin family he refers to all the girls as his sisters, and there was one in particular, their friend Ann Chappelle, who he included.

Flinders had applied to join *HMS Reliance* which was to take Governor John Hunter to New South Wales and to carry out exploratory work there. It is not known how it was that he was accepted, but it is likely that Admiral Pasley supported him, and Flinders had met Governor Hunter when Captain Bligh put into port in South Africa. However, it was probably largely due to the influence of Sir Joseph Banks who inherited Revesby Abbey, near Boston as a young man when his father died and to whom Flinders was known describing him as his fellow countryman. Sir Joseph was not only a wealthy man but well educated, having been at Christ Church, Oxford. He was interested in all scientific matters, particularly botany in which he first became interested at Eton when, returning from a walk by the Thames, he lagged behind his companions examining the wild flowers in the hedgerows.

He took part in an expedition to Newfoundland and made a considerable financial contribution (more than George III) to the costs of Cook's expedition in the *Endeavour* in 1768-1771, in which he took part after obtaining permission from his friend, the Earl of Sandwich, First Lord of the Admiralty. He had the privilege of being given the large cabin, where he was able to write, draw and keep plants. This resulted in Cook, who was six foot tall, having a small cabin just large enough for a bed and a desk, with a small wash basin outside in the passage. It was during that voyage that New South Wales was first sighted and the landing made at Botany Bay where a substantial number of plants was collected.

When he returned home he was regarded as an authority on New South Wales: he was made an Honorary Doctor of Civil Law at Oxford. Banks became scientific adviser to George III and a director of Kew Gardens and in 1778 was elected President of the Royal Society. Although he was to spend much of his time in London, he always remained interested in the affairs of Lincolnshire, particularly Boston, and he became a Freeman of the Borough.

For Flinders to volunteer to sail in the *Reliance* with such an expedition was no easy option, as, apart from the memory of Captain Cook's murder, unknown seas would be explored and great dangers and hardships faced over a long period. In this age we admire the courage and spirit of polar explorers and the astronauts, but at least they have communication with their base and many modern aids. The early seafarers, in their creaking and often leaking wooden ships, had no such support and knew that if they foundered they were lost.

Two ships, the *Reliance* and the *Supply* sailed from Plymouth on 15th February 1795. At Tenerife on 6th March Flinders wrote to his group of young relatives with a note to "Miss Chappelle I sincerely thank you for your kind letter from Hull and hope you received mine in return". He also commented on the pleasantly warm climate, which was a contrast to the severe winter weather at Plymouth where they needed to wear double overcoats.

Wishing to avoid the French, the ships sailed to Rio de Janeiro before going to New South Wales, reaching Port Jackson on 7th of September 1795.

In January 1788 Governor Philip had written to Lord Sydney in London to say that having reached Botany Bay, where following the recommendation of Joseph Banks he had been ordered to set up a penal colony, he had found it unsuitable. Therefore, he had gone on to Port Jackson, behind which he had found "the finest harbour in the world in which a thousand sail of the line may ride in perfect security". He fixed on one cove which had a fine water supply and where ships could anchor near the shore and which he said he "honoured with the name of Sydney". Letters written at the time were headed "Sydney Cove, Port Jackson", which is why Flinders always used the latter name.

Flinders' companions on board the *Reliance* included Captain Henry Waterhouse, who had been a lieutenant in the *Bellepheron*, and George Bass from Boston who had been apprenticed to Mr Francis, a surgeon. Bass had "walked the wards" of Boston hospital before winning his surgeon's diploma. However, like Flinders, he had felt the call of the sea, and his mother, by then a widow, had bought him a share in a merchant ship: this was wrecked and so he entered the Navy as a surgeon. Governor Hunter in official dispatches described him as a young man of well informed mind and an active disposition.

Samuel Flinders was also on board, although only twelve years old. When his elder brother was on leave in Donington, Samuel had begged him to take him to sea, and Matthew promised to look after him. Their father agreed with reluctance, it having been explained that if he joined so young, he would be eligible for promotion at an early age. Flinders had regretted that he had not gone to sea when he was that age. Their father must have been glad to learn from a letter written in Tenerife saying the boy was standing up well to the life, and after a letter from Rio de Janeiro, he recorded that he had heard from "my little Saml."

Captain Waterhouse undertook to take home Bennelong, an Aborigine, who together with a younger man Yemmerrawannie, had been brought to England in 1792. They were both presented to the King, but sadly Yemmerrawannie had died. Bennelong was not in good health, disliking the English climate, but he improved in the warmer sea air and with the care given him by George Bass, to whom he taught the Port Jackson language.

At Rio they spent several weeks taking on fresh supplies and resting the crew and where Flinders took the opportunity to make observations and draw sketches of the harbour. One of the lieutenants left the ship and Flinders was appointed acting lieutenant in his place.

As if the voyage was not enough, within a few weeks of the arrival at Port Jackson George Bass and Matthew Flinders volunteered to make short voyages along the coast which had only been explored for some fifteen miles north and twelve miles south of the harbour. Cook had produced a chart but there was little detailed knowledge, particularly about whether some of the rivers which inland explorers had seen were navigable down to the sea. There were no boats that could be used except those belonging to the ship, which were wanted, and they were told that rowing was too dangerous.

Flinders wrote "the furore of discovery, upon whatever

scale it is, is perhaps as strong, and can overlook obstacles, as well as most other kinds of mania. We turned our eyes towards a little boat of about 8 foot keel and 5 foot beam, which had been brought out by Mr Bass and others in the *Reliance* and from its size had obtained the name of *Tom Thumb*. In this boat we embarked on October 26th, which was the morning after our resolution had been formed". They took with them Bass's boy servant, William Martin, and were fortunate enough to get into Botany Bay on the ninth day, after "completely fulfilling the object of the excursion, by having traced the river some miles beyond where even the *Tom Thumb* would go". They reported on the good soil in the neighbourhood and as a result the settlement of Banks Town was established.

Although keen to explore further, another expedition was delayed as the *Reliance* was ordered to sail for Norfolk Island, a convict colony which was dependant on supplies being delivered at regular intervals, so it was not until March 1796 that a voyage could be planned to a river south of Botany Bay which had been sighted by Henry Hacking on a "kangurro hunting exercise".

Another boat of much the same size had been built and named *Tom Thumb* and in this they set off taking William Martin with them again and pushing "from between the heads with a breeze at WSW and set the sail" but soon were becalmed. They discovered that the drinking water had been put into a wine barica by mistake and was "exceedingly bad". Fortunately they had some water melons with them. Having spent the night on a rock they rowed south, hoping to pick up a breeze and when they recognised part of the coast which they had sighted while returning from Norfolk Island, they pushed into the shore at sunset. But there was too much surf to land: a "miserable supper was eaten" and they passed the night "as well as three people may be supposed to do in so small a space as the bottom of the *Tom Thumb*".

In the morning they still could not land, and were much in need of water, but decided to go on. After two and a half miles the coast was lower and beautifully green and there were beaches in between stoney heads. Seeing a place where there was less surf they tried to land. Bass threw the barrel over, leapt after it, and swam ashore. "On hauling the boat out again, our anchor, or stone, not being sufficiently heavy came home and before we could get it up to pull further out, a huge sea rose further out than usual, took the boat on its back and landed us on the beach nearly full of water". There was no time to be lost and they ran the boat out of the reach of the sea taking everything out, baling her dry. They were anxious to be gone quickly, as they could see smoke in the distance, and the native population south of Botany Bay were believed to be cannibals. With great difficulty they got the supplies back and relaunched the boat.

> Our condition was now as follows — three days of bread entirely spoiled; five days flour, not in the least wet; tea and coffee spoiled; sugar half wet; a few cakes of portable soup not much worse; one piece and a half of salt beef and three of pork; six pounds of rice and a little sago, good; the guns, rusty and full of sand and salt water, the rods incapable of being drawn; a barica of water, brackish; our clothes completely soaked; a watch and pocket compass, wet; one horn of powder, dry; and two wet; and a small bundle of wet sticks.

They approached one or two islands in the area of the cliff Flinders named Saddle Point, but it was impossible to land anywhere safe to dry out and "night now began to make its appearance, with its concomitant cold; which in our wet condition, was a very unwelcome visitor". Any sleep was difficult especially for Bass who had spent five hours naked in the water in the heat of the day, and was "now almost one continual blister". Next morning, Sunday 27th March, they heard voices calling them in the Port Jackson dialect offering them food and fresh water. They exchanged this for a few potatoes, which they had found wedged in the bottom boards of the boat, and two pocket handkerchiefs. The men said they were not natives of the place, having come from Rokeham and Botany Bays, but had been in Port Jackson, so both Bass and Flinders were able to understand some words at least of their language.

They landed at a nearby cove and managed to cook some food and dry their clothes, and the two natives followed them over the cliff. It was essential to find a good supply of water to fill the barica and the natives offered to take them to a river along the coast where they said they would also find duck and fish. They all squeezed into the boat and reached the point where a small stream had made a passage across the beach, and it was with difficulty they got the boat in and rowed a mile up in very shallow water against a strong current. The two natives walked, and were joined by about ten others.

Flinders and Bass were concerned that if the natives became hostile, it would be very difficult to get away, but nevertheless they went ashore to dry their powder, put the guns in order, mend an oar, and importantly get fresh water. The natives wanted them to fetch it from a large lake, but they thought it unwise to leave the boat, or to separate from each other, and after a while persuaded the natives to fetch water. They did this from a spring nearby which made Flinders suspicious as to why they were so anxious for them to go up to the lake. More natives arrived, and some appeared hostile so Flinders, having cut the hair and the beards of the first two previously, offered to do the same for the others. They had never seen scissors and Flinders describes the scene as they presented their faces as "not unworthy the pencil of Hogarth".

Bass had completed the repair of the oar, and they loaded their things back into the boat, hoping to get away peaceably, but the natives seemed to be insisting they go up to the lake, and the two from Port Jackson were showing signs of violence. Flinders told them that they would go there tomorrow, and said they would sleep on the green bank near the entrance of the river. They all started shouting and crying and shoving, but were persuaded to let go and Flinders dropped the anchor on the edge of the surf where the flow was too strong for them to follow. They kept hovering however, and Dilba, one of the Port Jackson men, constantly "importuned us to return and go up to the lagoon". It so happened that twelve months later he speared the chief mate and the carpenter of the ship *Sydney Cove*, so perhaps Flinders and Bass were right to be so apprehensive. They got away when the tide rose after dark, thinking that possibly the natives may have thought they were soldiers as Bass had a red waistcoat and they called him "soja".

At one in the morning they anchored off a small group of islands which they called Martin's Isles, and after dark the next evening they moved off in a fresh breeze. Having seen a gap in a reef they went through and found a sheltered beach where they cooked some food, and were able to sleep the night on the shore. "Perhaps the softest bed of down was never more enjoyed than was the fine sand of the beach by us at this time. The liberty of lying in any posture, stretching out our limbs was an indulgence which our little boat, with all her good qualities, could not afford: but I ought to have had a back covered with one continuous blister, to describe the condition of my companion". Refreshed and breakfasted they left this "friendly little place" to get away northwards. The wind freshened and they made little headway and pulled into a cove where they saw lumps of coal, where a stratum of coal was later found.

As the wind dropped they set off again but the sky became overcast with the wind continually veering. Flinders then describes the ensuing severe storm. With the moon behind heavy cloud all they could see was the grim cliffs and hear the thundering surf: water threatened to swamp the boat, and they thought they could only last another ten minutes. They were alongside a reef but had no idea what lay the other side, but as their situation was desperate, they pushed towards it and finding it did not run along the coast got under the lea of it and in three minutes were in smoother water in a cove with a beach. They named it Providential Cove although the native name was Watta-Mowlee, a name which Flinders used later. By nine next morning they were able to leave and by noon had reached Port Hacking where they made a meal and amused themselves in the evening with fishing "but the sharks were so numerous that no other fish dared make its appearance. The sharks were sufficiently daring to come to the surface eyeing us at the same time with voracious keen eyes".

Natives had visited them in the afternoon and were very civil. They understood each other tolerably well and Flinders had no sense of apprehension, saying that if it had not been for the mosquitoes they would have passed a comfortable night. They spent the day here and another night but did not think it would prove suitable as a port for shipping, so next morning, 1st April, they headed back to Port Jackson and by sunset arrived on board the *Reliance* in Sydney Cove.

In his understated manner he said that "although the

addition of knowledge gained did not deserve a particular narrative, some unlooked for circumstances occurred which rendered it somewhat interesting". Flinders called the account of this venture "Narrative of Tom Thumb's Cruize 1796".[1]

* * *

Most of the ships used for exploration were old, the Navy having to keep better equipped ships for fighting service. The *Reliance* was no exception, and on arrival at Port Jackson she was patched up and then accompanied again by the *Supply* set sail for South Africa by way of Cape Horn. Whilst there Flinders was able to take the examination in January 1797 so that his promotion to lieutenant could be confirmed, but the purpose of the voyage was to buy livestock so that the new colony at Sydney would begin to become self-sufficient. At the suggestion of Joseph Banks a supply of vegetables and seeds had been brought out from England but a supply of farm animals was needed. They brought back 109 cattle, 107 sheep, and 3 mares. Conditions must have been appalling and Captain Waterhouse described the voyage as one of the longest and most disagreeable passages he had ever made, getting back to Sydney in June 1797. Nevertheless, the animals they brought back were the foundation of Australia's livestock — particularly the Merino sheep. During the voyage across the Indian Ocean a litter of kittens was born. One of them was black with four white paws and a white star on his chest and was adopted by Flinders who called him Trim. Was it the turbulent voyage that was to make him into the adventurous cat that he became?

---

[1] The original is owned by the Flinders family who have given permission to quote from it, but it is on loan to the National Maritime Museum, Greenwich. A copy of it was made by Flinders' grandson, William Flinders Petrie, and was given to Melbourne Public Library in 1877.

The *Supply* was beyond repair and had only been brought back through the skill and courage of her commander, Lieutenant William Kent, but further repairs were needed to the *Reliance* and it was Flinders who was required to supervise them, so he was not able to take part in local exploration.

Bass, however, as the ship's surgeon, although he also worked in the hospital, had lighter duties and could be spared. He made one inland trip to seek a way across the great mountain barrier to the west because if the colony was to prosper, it needed to find more land where crops could be grown and cattle raised. The towering walls and great chasms of the Blue Mountains defeated him and the venture was unsuccessful. It was not until 1813 that a way was found.

The Governor then allowed him to take a whale boat with a crew of six to sail southwards again along the coast. They took provisions sufficient for six weeks, but in fact by fishing and shooting duck they extended this time to eleven weeks, leaving Port Jackson on 3rd December 1797 and returning on 25th February 1798. During this time they had sailed 300 miles beyond the point sighted by James Cook, or the coastline seen by Tobias Furneaux, and along what we now know as the Victoria Coast to Western Port, so named as it was the furthest point west that Bass could go.

On the 21st December they were held up because of a storm which lasted nine days and although they were able to explore the land, they found country with poor soil and covered in brushwood and ferns. Apart from the difficulty in making observations in an open boat, often in rough seas, Flinders later said that he believed Bass's quadrant had been damaged on the 31st December as his measurements were frequently ten miles out.

Bass made an attempt to sail south to the Furneaux Islands, but he had to alter course because the boat began to leak and they had a very rough and perilous journey back towards the mainland through the night. The following day, whilst looking for a sheltered bay, they saw several people on a small island. To Bass's surprise they were Europeans — seven convicts who had escaped from Port Jackson and had also been trying to head for the Furneaux Islands. While they were sleeping on the island at night, their companions had slipped away, obviously thinking there were too many in the boat. Bass, wanting to continue further, promised to come back. He sailed on to Western Port where storms kept him for thirteen days. Here they were able to shoot and salt a quantity of petrels to eat on the homeward voyage, but supplies were running low so reluctantly he turned for home. Bass did not have the experience or knowledge to make detailed charts, but he made drawings, and because he was in a small open boat got far closer to the coastline than a ship could do and so was able to observe it closely.

There was more bad weather and Bass had to take shelter on Wilson's Promontory, which gave him the chance to examine it, where he found no inhabitants and few birds although there was plenty of fresh water. He watched particularly the tides and wrote in his journal: "Whatever it shall be decided that the opening between this and Van Diemen's Land is a strait, this rapidity of tide, and the long south-west swell that seems to be continually rolling in upon the coast to the westward will then be accounted for". He was convinced that there was a strait, not only from the tides but also by the fact that the cliffs did not turn southwards and appeared to be buffeted by an open sea.

On February 2nd, keeping his promise to the convicts he took two of them back in the whale boat, one being old and the other clearly ill: the crew generously agreed to share their rations, although they were sparse enough. Unfortunately he could only take the others as far as the mainland giving them a musket, half his ammunition, fishing hooks, a cooking pot, and the best directions he could to make the long walk back to Port Jackson. They never arrived.

A foul east wind was encountered and Bass had to venture through heavy surf to take shelter on a beach before reaching Port Jackson at night.

Flinders, always interested in discoveries by others, wrote in his book many years later, "a voyage expressly undertaken for discovery in an open boat, and in which 600 miles of coast, mostly in a boisterous climate, was explored, has not, perhaps its equal in the journals of maritime history. The public will award to its high spirited and able conductor, alas! now no more, an honourable place in the list of those whose ardour stands most conspicuous for the promotion of useful knowledge".

Repairs completed to the *Reliance*, Flinders asked to carry out an exploration himself and got permission to join the schooner *Francis* as a passenger. She was about to sail to the Furneaux Islands, where it was known that the merchant ship, the *Sydney Cove,* had been driven ashore. Whilst some of her crew had with difficulty, and in a state of exhaustion, got back to Port Jackson in a boat, six of them had had to stay and a rescue operation to save them and her cargo was quickly organised.

Following the coast-line past which Cook had sailed Flinders was able to make more detailed observations, but he found the ship's compass was not very accurate. Flinders only had twelve days on the Furneaux Islands, but he made detailed notes about birds, animals and vegetation, as well as watching the tides, and at the same time as Bass was forming his opinion, Flinders felt certain that there was a large strait, confirmation of which would be of great importance. Shortly afterwards Bass and Flinders planned to make this exploration together.

* * *

Flinders had to return to duty, and was away from May to July when the *Reliance* was required to go to Norfolk Island again with urgently needed supplies and in August he sat as a member of the Admiralty Court to try a case of mutiny. Eventually, Governor Hunter, who was as keen as Flinders and Bass to discover if a passage existed between the mainland and the north coast of what today is called Tasmania, agreed that Flinders should take command of the sloop *Norfolk*.

The sloop was only in Sydney because the commandant of Norfolk Island, having had no contact with the mainland for over a year, commissioned her building and sent her to Sydney to urge immediate supplies. On arrival in Sydney, Hunter confiscated her, as the commandant had been ordered not to build any vessel that would be large enough for convicts to use for escape. She was built of pine, unsuitable for heavy seas and quarters were very cramped. Of course, she leaked.

Flinders, now age 24, found himself in command of a ship with official orders to sail and if a strait were found "to pass through it and return by south of Van Diemen's Land". The name changed to Tasmania to honour the Dutch navigator Abel Tasman who had first sighted the island. Flinders must have known that survival depended on his expert seamanship, but for him and for Bass it was a challenge which if successful would give them a place in history.

A crew of eight volunteers from the King's ships was found. Sadly there is only a record of two of their names, Simpson and John Thistle. Captain Waterhouse of the *Reliance* helped with the provision of equipment and stores but they were not permitted to take a chronometer to help calculations. Probably the few instruments available were thought too precious to risk in a vessel about 35 feet in length and 11 feet in beam, but it would have helped to be able to make accurate measurements in the difficult conditions with which they had to contend, and it was something Flinders regretted. They were ready to sail on 7th October 1798 and were to head for the Furneaux Islands and then the northern coast of Van Diemen's Land. On the way south along the mainland coast, taking a break from what is described as a foul wind, (an expression frequently used) to carry out a land survey, Flinders recorded an amusing incident at Two-Fold Bay.

> Our attention was suddenly called by the screams of three women, who took up their children and ran off in great consternation. Soon after a man made his appearance. He was of middle-age, unarmed except with a whaddie or wooden scimitar, and came up to us seemingly with careless confidence. We made much of him and gave him some biscuit: and he in return presented us with a piece of grizzly fat, probably of whale. This I tasted; but watching an opportunity to spit it out when he should not be looking, I perceived him to be doing precisely the same thing with our biscuit, whose taste was probably no more agreeable to him than his whale meat to me. Walking onward with us to the Long Beach, our new acquaintance picked up from the grass a long wooden spear pointed with bone, this he hid a little further on making signs that he should take it on his return. The commencement of our trigonometrical operations was seen by him with indifference, if not

> contempt; and he quitted us, apparently satisfied that, from people that could thus occupy themselves seriously there was nothing to be apprehended.

A day later a group of young men came down from the woods to watch them. They were offered some small presents, but clearly were more interested in the equipment and the European style of dress.

The *Norfolk* was able to sail again on 14th October, keeping the coast in sight, as Flinders never missed a chance to carry out surveys and give detailed descriptions of every hill, inlet or open space. He headed for the Kent group, which he had previously discovered when he visited the Furneaux Islands and which he had named after the brave captain of the *Supply* who had brought that unseaworthy ship back from South Africa.

On October 18th he sighted a large piece of hilly land which, thinking of Ann, he named Mount Chappelle, and then continued on to the Furneaux Islands and the north coast of Van Diemen's Land as far as the river now known as the Tamar. Here they stayed a month, carrying out a survey and being held up again by very bad weather until 3rd December.

The manner in which the coast then ran northwards made Flinders and Bass think that there might after all be no navigable strait. The water seemed discoloured and he thought that they were entering a wide bay with the coast running up to the mainland, but on the 7th December he wrote that "the tide had been running eastward all the afternoon and contrary to expectation we found it to be near low water on the shore: the flood therefore came from the west and not from the eastward as at the Furneaux Isles." This he considered strong proof, "not only of the real existence of a passage betwixt this land and New South

Wales, but also that the entrance to the Southern Ocean could not be far distant."

Shortly afterwards they went through what they were certain was a very wide strait and it does not take much imagination to think of the excitement of those ten men out alone in the expanse of sea, which at Flinders' suggestion when they returned to port, and with Governor Hunter's blessing, was to become known as the Bass Strait. Flinders always wrote Bass's Strait. This was an example of Flinders' generosity and his not wishing always to seek the limelight: it was right because it had been George Bass's expedition in the whale boat that had convinced the Governor that there was a definite possibility that a strait existed.

Turning to the south they sailed past the west coast of Van Diemen's Land, the little ship standing up remarkably well to the large swells. The man from the flat fenlands of England was amazed and perhaps fearful.

> The mountains which presented themselves to our view in this situation, both close to the shore and inland, were amongst the most stupendous works of nature I ever beheld, and it seemed to me are the most dismal and barren that can be imagined. The eye ranges over these peaks, and curiously formed lumps of adamantine rock, with astonishment and horror.

Calling the headland Cape Grim he put on all sail to get past this stretch of coast speedily, the sheer face of the cliffs making him realise that if a sudden storm blew up the *Norfolk* would have been in danger of being dashed against them, and adding that from its appearance the west coast of Van Diemen's Land was "as dreary, and as inhospitable a shore as has yet been discovered".

As their voyage continued southwards he named Mount

Zeehan and Mount Heemskirk after Tasman's two ships, believing them to be the mountains seen by Abel Tasman in 1642. By 13th December they had rounded the south west corner of the island and had encountered a very severe storm. It lasted only about an hour and came from the west: had it come from the south Flinders wrote that probably they would have been driven ashore and would not have survived.

The southern coast had been visited by a number of explorers, including Tasman, Cook and Bligh, and at Adventure Bay, young Flinders had gone ashore on the way to Tahiti in the *Providence*. On 21st December they reached the Derwent Estuary, where they surveyed the area, and as a result of the favourable report made, the first settlement of Hobart began four years later. Flinders would have found it hard to believe that within some thirty six years the settlement supported an elegant theatre, which is still in existence, the building being older than any theatre building in London.

As ever, Bass seemed to have boundless energy and enthusiasm, wanting to explore inland and make notes on the country, its soil, birds and animals. On Christmas Day he was the first European to climb what is now known as Mount Wellington, rising behind Hobart, and see the view of the surrounding mountainous country, the islands and the great deep harbour, and out to the open sea, beyond which there is no land until Antarctica.

The only contact they had with members of the native population took place in the Derwent area. Voices were heard calling from a hill: Bass and Flinders landed and took with them a swan as an offering of friendship. They met a man and two women, but the women ran away. The man stayed, gladly accepted the swan and although he was carrying three spears, he was friendly. They tried to speak to him in the language used in New South Wales, but he couldn't understand although Flinders noted that he quickly understood their signs. They left him "delighted with the certain possession of his swan".

They had been away longer than orders decreed, and in spite of some fishing and shooting, supplies were running low, so on 1st January 1799 they headed for Port Jackson. The winds made it difficult to do any serious survey, but they reported on the vast number of sea birds, and Bass wrote that he saw some 300 black swans in a space of a quarter of a mile square.

Arrived back at Port Jackson on 12th January and anchored alongside the *Reliance*, they must have felt a moment of great triumph, but Flinders was not a man to be idle. Apart from returning to normal duties, reports had to be made which Governor Hunter sent back to London: these brought Flinders to the notice of the Admiralty and of Sir Joseph Banks, as no such significant discovery had been made since the days of Captain Cook. It was a high point in Flinders' life.

* * *

For the second time he was required to sit as a member of a judicial court in a case that received a great deal of attention. A former convict, Isaac Nichols, who had made good and prospered was accused of receiving a basket of tobacco knowing that it was stolen. The community was split in its opinion, with the Governor convinced that Nichols had been set up by those jealous of his success and the Judge Advocate insisting that Nichols was guilty. The court consisted of six officers: three from the Army; three from the Navy, the latter being Waterhouse, Kent and Flinders who were all convinced of the prisoner's innocence, but were outvoted by the Army officers and the Judge Advocate. The latter was what was known as a remittance man, that is to say he was paid an allowance by his family to keep him away from England, and he was disliked by the Governor.

Flinders could have shrugged his shoulders, but he could not let this rest and drew up a skilfully worded paper in the defence. In the end sentence was suspended and Nichols was later granted a pardon by the Crown, although because of the slow communication it did not arrive until 1802.

* * *

As the great range of the Blue Mountains blocked the way into the interior, it was thought that other ways might be discovered, possibly by finding navigable rivers along the banks of which settlements might be founded and land cultivated. Flinders, like many others was interested in finding out what lay beyond the coastal fringe of this vast and new land, and he volunteered to undertake an expedition. The *Reliance* at that time had no specific duties and the Governor agreed that the *Norfolk* could be used, but only for a period of six weeks. It was the season of the year when severe winter storms could be expected and therefore it was inadvisable for the expedition to go through the Bass Strait, beyond Western Point (the furthest point which Bass had reached) and on to the great unknown southern coast. It was, therefore, agreed that the *Norfolk* should be taken up the eastern coast to the areas of Moreton Bay and Hervey Bay, both of which Cook had named but had not entered.[2]

This time Captain Waterhouse allowed a chronometer from the *Reliance* to be taken. As George Bass had left the *Reliance* and gone home, Flinders took with him his

---

[2] Cook named it Morton Bay but because of a printing error it became known as Moreton Bay.

younger brother, Samuel, and a native of Sydney Cove, Bonargee, "whose good disposition and manly conduct" attracted him as it was thought he would be helpful when approaching local people, and he also took his cat, Trim. The rest of the crew were the men who had been through the Bass Strait the previous December.

The *Norfolk* left Port Jackson on 8th July, 1799, but two days later, in a foul wind, the sloop was leaking so badly that it was necessary to find a beach where she could be heaved down and repairs made. Flinders took the sloop's boat in among some sandbanks to try to find a suitable place, but he did not realise that this was the estuary of a sizeable river (later called the Clarence River) which was oozing its way to the sea through narrow channels between shoals covered in vegetation and inhabited by noisy parakeets and cockatoos. He called the place Shoal Bay, saying that it was an appellation that was well merited. There was no suitable beach to bring in the ship, but the sailors had found a loose plank and made a temporary repair, so they were able to sail on northwards, and into Moreton Bay. From here they could see one of the peaks arising sharply from flat land that Cook had named the Glass Houses as their curious formations seen from the sea reminded him of the glass making factories of his native Yorkshire.

It was near the entrance to Moreton Bay that some native inhabitants were encountered. The meeting began in a friendly way, but on being offered gifts, one of them wanted to take Flinders' straw hat, and when this was refused they threw a spear at the boat, which fortunately missed the men. The natives continued to appear aggressive, so a musket shot was fired and they retreated into the undergrowth. Flinders named the place Skirmish Point.

A few miles further up a small river, which was named the Pumice-stone River because of the nature of the rocks, a place was found where the ship could be unloaded safely and more adequate repairs made. That achieved, Flinders, Bonargee and two sailors took the small boat upstream for a couple of miles and then scrambled over rocks and through undergrowth for nine hours until they reached the nearest peak which they succeeded in climbing. Here they spent the night, but were not able to attempt a second peak which rose in a perpendicular wall in front of them. They had a view of the other strange rock formations and the mountains beyond before returning to the boat and gliding back to where the *Norfolk* waited for them to take them back to the sea.

Again they sailed on northwards making for Hervey Bay and examining the coast before turning southwards for the return voyage. Held up by a contrary wind they met another group of natives, but this time it was a friendly encounter, and they arrived back in Port Jackson safely, six weeks and one day after they had left.

Flinders was disappointed that he had not succeeded in finding a navigable river into the interior and was later to write that however mortifying this was "it was then an ascertained fact that no river of importance intersected the East Coast between the 24th and 39th degrees of latitude". He was never to know that he was wrong and that he had missed the estuaries of two large rivers, the Clarence and the Brisbane.

* * *

Another supply run was made to Norfolk Island before the *Reliance* sailed for England, Governor Hunter having decided that she must make the voyage back while still in sufficient repair. It was a stormy voyage and the ship leaked so badly that she made about nine inches of water every hour. Luckily for the crew two convicts had stowed away, emerging after two days out of Sydney and were put to work manning the pumps.

3

Servant of the Sea

Flinders had for sometime been concerned about his future and he had considered leaving the Navy and joining George Bass in trading ventures. Trading in the East seemed more attractive than spending his life on poor pay and dependant on patronage for promotion, but Bass did not seem to wish to enter into a trading partnership.

Bass and Flinders were never to meet again. George Bass had gone home separately and married Elizabeth Waterhouse, sister of Captain Waterhouse. After only a few weeks he had sailed again and arrived back in Sydney with a cargo of goods, which he had difficulty in selling, partly because more trading ships were coming over from England, the colony was beginning to produce food and it seems that the Governor was going through a period of economy. He made one or two trips to Tahiti to collect salted pork and then followed a somewhat mysterious voyage, albeit with an official recommendation from the Governor, which was intended to take him to Chile to sell the remainder of his original cargo. It is a tragedy that he never returned, and no-one knows what became of him.

Thinking about his future on his twenty fifth birthday and yearning to see Ann again Flinders wrote a long letter to her from Port Jackson in which he said:-

Sea, I am thy servant, but my wages must afford me more than a bare subsistence. I do not mean to be alway insulted. Thou art but a rough master, hast little mercy

upon the lives and limbs of thy followers, but sometimes
thou bestowest favours. Half my life I would dedicate
to thee, but the whole I cannot if thou keepest me in
penury all the morning and noon of life.

Yet after the six months voyage home one of the first
things he did, and still aboard the *Reliance*, was to write to
Sir Joseph Banks about the exploration of the southern
coast. No one knew what lay there or if New South Wales
and New Holland were separated by a sea.

Although a small sloop, *The Lady Nelson*, had recently
been sent out, Flinders wrote on the 6th September 1800
"If Sir Joseph Banks would excuse me I presume she must
be very inadequate to the task, as perhaps would any single
vessel". Knowing the French were also interested in the
area, he felt no time should be lost and begged that a larger
ship should be found, which he offered to command.

Although Flinders' name and his achievements were well
known in England because some of his charts had been
sent home already, it was a quite unheard of thing for a
young lieutenant to write in such a manner to someone so
distinguished, but Flinders knew that Banks was considered
an authority on what little was known of Terra Australis
and that he was generous in helping young men keen to
increase botanical knowledge. It was several weeks before
a reply was received and Flinders may have felt anxious
that he would be dismissed. In fact some time before
Banks had written to Mungo Park, well known for his
explorations in West Africa, to ask him if he would go
out to Terra Australis in a ship which he intended to ask
the Admiralty to make available under the command of
Matthew Flinders. Mungo Park had declined as having
recently married he did not wish to go off on further
exploration at that time. The delay in the reply was caused
by Flinders' letter having to be forwarded from Banks'

London address and the fact that Banks was ill.

Flinders' approach was bold, but it was right. Banks wrote to the King and Earl Spencer and on 12th December 1800 the Admiralty issued an order to prepare for the voyage realising the urgency because the French Government had already applied for a passport for two ships, under the command of Captain Nicolas Baudin, to carry out exploratory work. Although France and Britain were at war, both governments encouraged and respected those who undertook voyages of scientific discovery. Passports were issued and should ships meet, their captains were under orders to act towards each other as though their countries were not at war. Just as George III was interested in scientific discovery, so was Napoleon. Nevertheless, there was bound to be a certain rivalry as both nations were looking to extend their interests in trading and possible colonisation in the new lands which they knew existed. In the case of Terra Australis a race was now on to get there first.

HMS Xenophon was chosen, her name being changed to the *Investigator*. She was a ship which had been bought by the Admiralty and used for convoy duties.

On the 19th day of January 1801, a commission was signed by the Lords Commissioners of the Admiralty for Lieut. Matthew Flinders to be lieutenant of His Majesty's ship the *Investigator*, and he immediately took command. On the 25th January his commission was read on board the ship, then lying in the harbour of Sheerness.

She was lately out of dock, having been coppered, and was now new rigged, but had nothing on board but some men and shingle ballast, and few provisions.

An application to the Navy Board was made to order the officers of the yard to provide stores without reference to the usual mode of fitting of ships of war, but leaving this to Flinders' judgment.

Flinders was to be promoted Commander on the 16th February, one of the youngest ever to be given that rank. Neither Bligh nor Cook was promoted in this way at the outset of their first voyages.

Built on similar lines to Cook's ship the *Endeavour,* Flinders was pleasantly surprised at the spaciousness of the Captain's cabin with its fireplace for use in cold weather, its long table on which work on charts and drawings could be carried out, and with the sleeping quarters, the latter being similar to those which had been occupied by Joseph Banks. The other officers had small cabins, not much larger than cupboards, as did such men as the boatswain and the carpenter, but the rest of the crew slept in the hammocks suspended from the beams. Chests were nailed to the flooring to provide storage space, each man having the use of half a chest in which to store his clothing. The lids were the benches on which to sit at table for meals. A large iron stove was used for cooking, which must have made the quarters unbearable in hot weather, but near which clothing was probably dried off in wet weather. She was considered suitable to withstand the weather conditions that would be met. Some of the guns were removed, which gave more space, but it did have the effect of weakening the structure, which was to prove a problem. There were other defects which had been overlooked in the haste: inner timbers, concealed by the copper lining were rotten and this was to be the cause of the ship leaking badly. In time of war the best ships had to be kept for active service and Flinders was to write later:

> The leakiness of the ship increased with the continuance of the south west wind, and at the end of a week amounted to five inches of water an hour .... Should

it be asked why representations were not made and a stronger vessel procured, I answer that the exigencies of the Navy were such at that time that I was given to understand no better ship could be spared from the service; and my anxiety to complete the investigation of the coasts of Terra Australis did not admit of refusing the one offered.

The sad truth is that ships used for exploration were often not as sound as they should have been. They had to be fairly small to enable them to get near the coast, and they had to withstand voyages across the world's seas, but they had often been built for other purposes, then patched up and partially re-constructed. Both Cook's ship the *Endeavour* and Flinders' ship the *Investigator* had originally been used for carrying coal in coastal waters. As late as 1846, Thomas Huxley wrote of the condition of *HMS Rattlesnake*, sent out to survey further the Great Barrier Reef, saying that ships used for exploration were invariably found to be the clumsiest and most inconvenient ships to wear the pennant. "In accordance with the rule, such was the *Rattlesnake* and to carry out the spirit of the authorities more completely, she was turned out of Plymouth dockyard in such a disgraceful state of unfitness, that the lower deck was continually underwater during the voyage."

In preparing for the voyage in snowy January weather Flinders followed the example of Captain Cook and paid particular attention to the supply of food, taking seven months' supply of dry provisions, stressing the need for antiscorbutics — that is to say limes and lemons to counteract scurvy which so often afflicted sailors on long voyages, causing severe disability and even death. Some fresh food was taken on the start of the voyage and some pigs and sheep to be killed and eaten, but the daily diet had to consist mainly of salted pork and beef, occasionally onions, and ship's biscuits which had to be baked several times during the voyage to kill off the weevils. Sauerkraut, vinegar, sugar and what was called portable soup, made by boiling meat and bones and forming a dry powder, was carried. Modern tests have found that this soup contained little nutrition, but it did provide a hot drink. Particular attention was paid to the water supply. Sixty tons were taken on board, Flinders insisting that the casks were new. After his experiences sailing with Captain Bligh he never restricted the supply of drinking water.

On Tuesday 5th May a letter was written to the Agent Victualler at Chatham, complaining of the shortness of weight in the fresh beef, which had been 20lbs short in March, 39 short in April and was now 9lbs short and he asked that a caution might be given to the boatmen. The answer came back that the master of the brig would take oath, that none had ever been cut off in his vessel; that the quarters were weighed in the presence of three clerks, and not until the beef was cold. The letter had some effect for the next consignment was 5lb greater than charged.

On the same day Flinders wrote to the Admiralty requesting them to order the *Investigator* to be paid six months wages; the resident Commissioner objected to payments being made until sailing orders had arrived, but the Admiralty agreed to the request. Another letter was sent to the Navy Board requesting them to stop the allotment of William Kemble, a Marine, and he was discharged as being a deserter from the Inniskilling or 6th Dragoon Regiment.

At the end of May a letter was sent to the Admiralty explaining that the guns now on board were more than sufficient to combat Indians, and that they prevented the taking on of sufficient water. Understanding that a passport was to be obtained and was now daily expected, Flinders asked that their Lordships would be pleased to order that ten of the twelve long six-pounders now on board should be taken out, and that instead the ship should be supplied with six twelve-pound carronades and two more swivels. These guns, in addition to the eighteen-pound carronades already on board, he considered to be sufficient to repel the attack of any Indians with whom they would be likely to meet. He also asked to be supplied with a pocket time piece.

Some armament had to be carried, surveying and astronomical instruments, timekeepers, and a supply of knives, mirrors and coloured cloth to use as gifts or for barter with native people. A quantity of scientific books was selected, paper for writing and for charts, new log books, ink and two thousand quill pens. Also loaded was a spare anchor, extra sails and a supply of ropes was essential for repairs to the 18 miles of rope used in the rigging with its 148 separate parts. Damaged rope was not wasted. It had to be shredded by hand and was used for repairing cracks in timbers. Lengths were hung up so that greasy hands could be wiped after meals and there being no lavatory paper it was also used for that purpose.

Joseph Banks was responsible for the civilians who were to travel. Robert Brown was chosen as the naturalist, to collect plants and to observe animals, and had been recommended by Banks' librarian. He had been trained in medicine at Edinburgh and was now serving as an Army surgeon in Ireland, but his interest in natural history had led him to visit Sir Joseph's herbarium when on leave in England. A somewhat reserved Scot, he was dedicated to his work and was eventually to become one of the most distinguished naturalists of his time.

An Austrian, whose father had been Court painter to the Prince of Liechtenstein, was appointed to undertake the drawings of the animals seen and the plants collected. His name was Ferdinand Bauer and whilst working in Vienna he was asked by John Sibthorp, a wealthy young man from Lincolnshire, to join him as an illustrator on the expedition he was making to Italy, Greece, Cyprus, Crete and Turkey as part of the Radcliffe Travelling Fellowship which he had been awarded. Bauer returned with him to Oxford to complete the drawings and later worked in London. Banks probably knew about his detailed and exceptionally beautiful drawings as not only must he have known Sibthorp's work, but it was Banks who had appointed Franz Bauer, Ferdinand's elder brother, to be chief botanical painter at Kew. In 1801 he was about forty years of age, considerably older than the others, but with his happy temperament he was to fit in well.

The appointment of a landscape painter proved difficult, but finally the position was offered to the younger brother of Richard Westall, a well known artist in his time. Young William Westall was only nineteen, a student at the Royal Academy School and seemingly given to practical jokes. Flinders wrote to Ann that "his foolish days are not yet passed". He made almost diagrammatic drawings of parts of the Australian coastline which would help in the recognition of its features and many paintings of scenery. The astronomer John Crosley was chosen by the Admiralty, the Board of Longitude and the Astronomer Royal, Sir Nevil Maskelyne. He had sailed on a surveying ship in the northern Pacific between 1795 and 1797 and had not been in a good state of health when he returned, so hesitated before accepting. Robert Brown was paid £420 a year, the others £315 and they were allowed to take a boy with them to look after their clothes and keep their cabins clean.

The gardener appointed to care for the plant collection was Peter Good, a foreman at Kew Gardens. He had already spent time at sea taking English plants to the East India Company's garden in Calcutta and returning with plants from India to grow at Kew. He was said to be quiet and gentle and was a most valuable assistant to Brown. John Allen was described as a practical miner and probably came from Sir Joseph Banks' estate in Derbyshire. His work was to look for mineral deposits in the rocks and soil and a better description of his role might be geological assistant to Robert Brown. They were paid £105 a year, and Banks said "These must rough it", though in fact they had better quarters than the ordinary seamen.

Discussions took place with the Sick and Hurt Board and Hugh Bell, recommended by the Navy's chief physician, was appointed as surgeon. Although he had an interest in botany and sometimes went ashore with the others, he had an abrupt manner which was irritating and he did not get on particularly well with the commander. An application had to be made to the Sick and Hurt Board for instructions concerning seamen who might have to be sent ashore in foreign parts.

The appointment of the officers and men was left to Flinders, and there was no shortage of applicants. Among the officers was Robert Fowler, who as First Lieutenant, had sailed in the ship when she had been on convoy duty and whose home was in Horncastle, Flinders' brother, Samuel, as Second Lieutenant and their cousin, John Franklin from Spilsby as a Midshipman. John Thistle, who had been with Bass in the whale boat and in the *Norfolk* when the Bass Strait was discovered, had just returned home after six years: he immediately volunteered, and on the 3rd June Flinders put in a request that he should be appointed Master and this was agreed.

Of the seamen, Flinders insisted that they should be volunteers. Too many ships had sailed with men who had been press ganged, and not surprisingly they had caused trouble. Many of the men came over from the *Reliance*: others from the crew of the *Zealand*, two hundred and fifty of whom lined up offering to go, and eleven were chosen.

There were several cats to act as rat-catchers and one or two dogs who were useful on hunting expeditions. And of course, there was Trim, born on board *HMS Reliance* and so already a veteran of the sea, who Flinders had taken with him to London, travelling on the seat of the coach, the favourite cat of the whole crew and about whom Flinders was to write so movingly.

On Tuesday 9th June orders were received to proceed into Portsmouth Harbour, to dock the ship and get her defects repaired with expedition and return to Spithead and also an order to send any men suspected of intending to desert on board the *Royal William*.

Flinders knew that he must sail as soon as possible, partly because the French expedition would now be on its way and partly to arrive in time to make the most of the better weather conditions. Therefore he frequently urged the need to speed up the preparations, to give him clear instructions and let him have the final orders to sail.

On the 19th June Flinders was ordered to go up to London to answer questions concerning the commander of a ship called the *Andersons* who had deserted the convoy of *HMS Reliance* in the previous September. He took the opportunity to go to the Admiralty in an attempt to forward the issue of his sailing orders, but this had little effect as what he described as the multiplicity of business prevented his voice being heard. A few days later *The*

Times reported that the *Investigator* was about to sail to Botany Bay and that she was admirably fitted out and manned by picked men. The "scientific gentlemen" as Flinders called them had joined the ship at Spithead and to fill in their time whilst waiting to sail they went over to the Isle of Wight and into the Hampshire countryside to look for plants.

On 2nd July a letter went to the Admiralty asking for instructions on the conduct to be observed should French ships be met, or ships of other nations with which the United Kingdom was at war. He also wrote that with the advancement of the seasons every day's delay in sailing would have bad consequence, meaning that the weather in the southern hemisphere would be deteriorating by the time they arrived, which would jeopardise the success of the expedition.

During the months the ship was waiting, both at the Nore and at Spithead Flinders wrote that he had endeavoured to bring the ship's company under good order and government, to which the majority of them responded, but occasionally some fell under the lash, though none of them showed any sign of an ill disposition towards the officers or to living sociably with each other. There had been some desertions so shore leave had been cancelled since the men had been paid.

On Friday 17th July the sailing orders were received together with thirteen pages of instructions and the passport from the French Republic to prevent the *Investigator* being molested and with permission to put into ports to refit if necessary on condition that no offence was given to the French or their allies. There were a number of other documents providing for the victualling of the astronomer, the naturalist and their servants and the gardener and the miner, together with a letter to the Governor of New South Wales concerning the *Lady Nelson*, the small ship recently sent out under the command of Lieutenant James Grant, and which it was proposed should be used as a supporting ship to the *Investigator*.

The weather is recorded as squally, with heavy rain, large hailstones, thunder and lightning.

By the next morning, however, it was cloudy with rain at times and a north westerly wind. Last minute loading of food and water took place. The purser's steward was missing as was one of the seamen, and because two others had had to be discharged, they were four men short of complement. In the journal it is recorded: "At 10, made the signal and weighed."

4

For Love of Ann

When he arrived home in the *Reliance* Flinders had also written immediately to Ann Chapelle in Lincolnshire, complaining he had no answers to letters written from New South Wales. It has to be remembered that the safe arrival of letters was not a certainty and also that it was considered somewhat improper for young women to indulge in correspondence with young men, unless engaged to them. Ann must have considered that it was fairly hopeless to think of an engagement when Flinders appeared to have no prospects and neither of them had independent means.

On 20th September 1800 Flinders wrote saying his imagination had flown to her frequently during the six years he had been away. He went on to say that when the ship was paid off he would go to London "to put the business I have got to do into fair training" and that he hoped to visit Lincolnshire.

> You see that I make everything subservient to business. Indeed, my dearest friend, this time seems to be a very critical period of my life. I have been long absent, have services abroad that were not expected, but which seem to be thought a good deal of. I have more and greater friends than before, and this seems to be the moment that their exertions may be the most serviceable to me. I may now perhaps make a bold dash forward, or remain a poor lieutenant all my life.

Ann was the daughter of John and Anne Chapelle, and she must have known of the hardships and separations of those who married sailors, her father having died at sea aged forty. He is said to have been a kind, well educated man known as the gentleman captain, and a great reader who like Flinders took his favourite book with him — in this case *Paradise Lost*.

Some time later, Mrs Chapelle married again, to the Reverend William Tyler, who owned a house in Partney although vicar of Braytoft, and a daughter, Isabella, was born, who was known affectionately as Belle. Although ten years younger, she and Ann were devoted to each other.

Even though these letters were written long ago, it still feels an intrusion to read them, but it is from them that we learn a great deal of the background to Flinders' life, and to that of Ann, and realise that he was a young man in love who was also driven by an almost missionary zeal to try to finish the task he had begun and which he was so highly qualified to do.

Letters went back and forth, Ann hoping that he might settle down, but had he done so promotion would have been unlikely and he could not afford to marry on the pay of a lieutenant, whereas the proposed return to New South Wales meant he would have immediate promotion. He did not want to return there without her and had even written to his father asking for a loan of £100 to help his expenses, but this was refused as his father had had some financial difficulties and, hoping to retire before much longer, he made it plain that he could not give any money at the present time. Ann's father took a kindly view and said he would let them have £100, and fortunately Flinders learnt that the three hundred acres of land at Banks Town, Botany Bay, granted to him by the Governor in January

1800 in recognition of his services, had been sold.

On 10th December, Matthew wrote that he had hopes to come to Lincolnshire with Sir Joseph Banks and begged Ann to be at Partney, saying he did not wish to return to New South Wales without her, but urging her to "learn more music, French and enlarge the subjects of thy pencil. Study geography and astronomy and even metaphysics sooner than leave thy mind unoccupied". He added that she should read anything except rubbishy novels.

He goes on to say that he "must call ambition to his assistance since it must be so; and in a life of activity and danger put out of my mind but that we are friends" but says that when in solitude he had vowed he would not return to New South Wales without a partner of his love. "How are human projects blasted!" He continues that he did not value her less for her want of fortune and that if he possessed £10,000 his hand would await her acceptance. As he is going to travel to Lincolnshire with Sir Joseph he hopes that by "personal conferences" they might come to a better understanding than by letter. "Let us meet as lovers and part as friends, my Annette. Ah me!"

Although they did meet, they must have had a tearful parting and it would seem that Matthew had explained to Ann that there was little prospect of marrying as on the pay of a Lieutenant he could not support her. He would appear to have said that it would be better to part and for her to marry another, as on 16th January 1801 he wrote from London:

> Excuse everything here, dear friend — tears are in my eyes — I am torn to pieces. Thou had promised to inform me when thou art married and I trust that the earliest opportunity afterwards will bring me the intelligence; it will be important to me. And whilst I am

torn by winds and waves of various coasts and in various climes, may thou enjoy that serenity that a contemplative mind feels on surveying its own happiness. May thou meet with one whose mind and heart is worthy of thy love and whose circumstances unlike mine, can afford thee the enjoyment of life. Adieu, perhaps the last time. This excess of misery is too great to be often recalled. It is seldom that I have written a letter in tears.

He wrote again on 27th January saying how desolate he felt. Clearly he realised that while he had occupations Ann had not. She must remember him as a friend as on love they must not think, although Ann had asked if there was not a "possibility of their living together". Concerned that it was because of him that she had not already married, he made a will leaving half his money to Ann if she was unmarried at the time of his death.

Having been given promotion in February Flinders was still trying to see a way in which he could marry Ann and take her with him on the voyage. On confirmation of his promotion he wrote on the 6th April saying he thought there was a probability of living together with a moderate share of comfort as he had accommodation on board the *Investigator*, "in which as my wife a woman may with love to assist her, make herself happy". As he would be in London for ten days or longer he asked if she would meet him there when "this hand shall be thine for ever". Even though he suggested Mr and Mrs Tyler accompany her, Ann thought it "indelicate". Poor Ann had been trying to return to the delights of friendship and at that time for a young woman of her background it would have been difficult indeed for her to return to Lincolnshire should her spirit have failed her when she arrived in London. The gossip in Partney can be imagined. Instead Matthew took the coach to Spilsby on the 15th April and they were married at the ancient church of St. Nicholas, Partney on the 17th, with the service taken by Mr Tyler. Isabella Tyler described the scene saying that of all the happy group none was more happy than the bridegroom. That evening Ann wrote to her friend Betsy Franklin, who was now a distant relative, telling her "I have given my hand at the altar to him I have ever highly esteemed" but expressing the pain she felt that she might never see Betsy again.

The following day, with Mr. Tyler's £100 put inside his boot for safety, Ann and Matthew, accompanied by Isabella, drove away in a post chaise. For a bride to take a sister, or other near relative was not an unusual custom, normally to help her settle in her new home. In this case Isabella was to help buy materials and have dresses made up for Ann to take with her.

They called at Donington and Matthew's father, not best pleased, wrote that his son had arrived "accompanied by a wife". By the 20th they were back in London: on the 27th Ann was aboard the *Investigator*, and Mr. Tyler, coming to London to preach a sermon for a missionary society, took Isabella to Sheerness to say farewell before escorting her back to Lincolnshire.

It was the intention that Ann should travel as far as Port Jackson, where she would be able to stay while her husband set off on voyages surveying the coast, but their happiness was to be short lived. In May the Lords of the Admiralty, unannounced, arrived to inspect the ship, where they found Ann in the Captain's cabin "without her bonnet" and therefore at home. Whether anything was said in front of her is not known but by the end of the month a letter from Joseph Banks was received which said he had just heard of the marriage and that the Admiralty was seriously displeased. He advised Flinders not to take

Ann on the voyage, and that if he did so it was likely that he would lose his command and the survey would be undertaken by someone else, probably Lieutenant Grant who was in command of *The Lady Nelson*, already in New South Wales.

It was not entirely unusual for a ship's captain to be allowed to have his wife on board in certain circumstances and although the Admiralty might not encourage it they either gave permission or turned a blind eye. Flinders replied to Banks that he had intended to take his wife, reminding him that Lieutenant King of the *Buffalo* had had his wife with him in New South Wales at the time when Flinders was there. In great agony of mind Flinders said that if the Admiralty insisted, he would leave her in England until he had completed the voyage of discovery and that "even this circumstance will not damp the ardour I feel to accomplish the important purpose of the present voyage and in a way that shall preclude the necessity of anyone following after me to explore". Banks, although he thoroughly disapproved of the marriage (he always disapproved of the marriages of the young men he helped) did offer to make a representation to the Admiralty, but it was no use.

Orders were received to take the *Investigator* from the Nore to Spithead, and Ann remained on board for the time being. At six o'clock on a fine evening the *Investigator* was sailing about four miles out to sea from Dungeness. Flinders was not on deck, but had indicated he would come out in half an hour's time. The seaman throwing the lead called out the depth of the water as fifteen fathoms just before the watch changed and it was not noticed that he had left his position before his relief took over. Within ten minutes the ship ground onto a sandbank. The fault lay with the leadsman, but the officer of the watch should have noticed. The commander rushed out to the quarter deck, the sails were thrown back and with a rising tide the ship was off the sandbank within two hours.

As no damage was done it was not strictly necessary to report it, but Flinders did so because he had not been given the accurate chart made only four years previously. Instead he had been issued with a chart which did not show this sandbank and he asked that the correct chart should be supplied in future so that other shipping could avoid it. Unfortunately there had been an earlier incident at the Nore when, having been ordered to let three men go to assist another ship, they absconded when they were recalled. Coupling the two incidents together the Admiralty complained that such things happened when the commander's wife was aboard. Some acrimonious letters were exchanged, Flinders fiercely complaining about such an insult to his wife.

With all the preparations for departure going on around her at Spithead, Ann, devastated by the thought of the parting that must happen, was making herself seriously ill. As a result when her husband was summoned to the Admiralty on 19th June he took her to London, leaving her in the care of friends. She certainly understood her husband's ambition but it is not difficult to understand her pain. In 1801 a girl of 28, who had not married was probably unlikely to do so, and would have had to resign herself to a quiet life in Lincolnshire, pleasant perhaps, but dull for a woman of her intelligence and dependant on her family. Clearly she had for a long time loved Matthew and had been swept off her feet when she saw him again — a brilliant and attractive man. She now had to accept returning to Lincolnshire for the years that Matthew would be away with the fear that he was now facing dangers from which he might not come back. She would have known that Cook had been murdered, that George Bass disappeared having sailed only a few months after his marriage to Elizabeth Waterhouse, and she would have known of the accidents and severe illness which afflicted so many explorers.

For Matthew it was also devastating. He wrote to a friend that he would not have married her unless he felt sure she could travel with him as other wives had done and he could not have foreseen that this privilege would be denied him. "Yet I am by no means sorry for having married. If you knew her worth you would not". To Ann he wrote "I am just as awkward as one half of a pair of scissors. The idea of how happy we might be will sometimes intrude itself and takes away the little spirits that my melancholy situation leaves me."

The routine work necessary for a ship in port had to continue but they exchanged letters almost daily and although his own sadness broke through he tried to cheer her. On the 5th July he wrote that he hoped that a very short period would see him back.

> Rest confident, my dear, of the ardent and unalterable affection of thine own MF: he <u>does</u> love thee beyond everything. I go, beloved, to gather riches and laurels with which to adorn thee; rejoice at the opportunity which fortune and circumstances give me to do it. Rest assured of the unalterable affection of <u>thine own</u> wanderer.

Later he wrote begging her to send him letters frequently.

> Tell me the dress thou wearest, tell me thy dreams, anything, so do but talk to me and of thyself. When thou art sitting at thy needle and alone, then think of me, my love, and write me the uppermost of thy thoughts. Fill me half a dozen sheets, and send them when thou canst.

Again he wrote to "his dearest girl" on 12th July after she had told him that her health was better saying that he still had no prospect of getting sailing orders, and asking if she would come back to Spithead where she could stay in a comfortable inn, or aboard ship — but adding that if her health did not permit this, she must take no risk. Her stepfather had already arranged to come down from Partney to take her home. Ann must have felt she could not face another parting and it was as well that she did not travel to Spithead, for sailing orders arrived on the 17th July. Flinders had a great task ahead of him however torn apart he felt. For Ann it was a long and lonely return to Lincolnshire.

In spite of all that was to happen they loved each other to the end of their lives.

5

The Investigator

After the long weeks of frustration waiting for the passport and final orders, the *Investigator* sailed at 10 o'clock on the morning of the 18th July 1801. The coast of England slipped away, the weather cleared and the long voyage began. Flinders later said that given what he called fortunate circumstances, there was nothing to record on such long voyages, but from his log book and his diary we do know something of the events of the journey.

The Articles of War having been read Flinders issued his own orders[1] on the afternoon of Sunday 19th July. They were long and detailed, concerning conduct during the voyage. The first part of the order was addressed to the boatswain, the gunner and the carpenter, stating that no stores should be issued without first applying to the commander. The second part was more lengthy and was addressed to the officers.

Detailed instructions to the officers of the watch were set out concerning the inspection of the sails, masts and rigging, the necessity of visiting frequently the person looking out, who was to be relieved each hour, or more often, and it was forbidden for anyone to speak to or distract the helmsman from the steerage of the ship.

Any material changes in the weather were to be reported to the commander and the officer was not to make any

---

[1] See Note 1

alteration of consequence to the sails without permission, except in the case of emergency. Detailed records had to be kept for inspection and an account given of the exact position of the ship at noon each day, to be shown to the Commander before one o'clock.

Flinders ended by stating that an officer must never lose sight of an order until not only the letter of it, but the spirit was fulfilled and that petty officers and men must not neglect any duty, much being expected of them. A day's work was expected from the midshipmen, who were also to record their own observations of latitude and longitude (the latter by any astronomical observation which they had mastered) and those who applied themselves would be allowed to work in the cabin and have help from the astronomer or the commander himself in the making of surveys and charts, so they were not only useful during the voyage but would lay a foundation for their future promotion.

Apart from Flinders' own journal, Robert Brown and Peter Good wrote journals and there was to be a voice from the lower deck as Seaman Samuel Smith also wrote an account in his unique style. He mentioned meeting four three-decked ships of the Grand Fleet and a few days later he wrote:

> At night we was piped all hands in the middle Watch to Quarters. A Brig was bearing down upon our Starboard Bow. Our Captn spoke her, but receiving no Answer we fired A Gun past his stern. Tackt Ship and spoke her, which prooved to be a Swede.

On 3rd August the *Investigator* reached Funchal, Madeira and a call was made on the Governor who gave permission for them to land, which allowed the botanists and artists a chance to work. A call was also made on the British Naval

Commandant: Portugal was our ally in the Napoleonic War, and British ships were allowed to use the harbour of Funchal. As the ship was already found to be leaking, the ship's timbers were checked and re-caulked by pushing oakum, made from old rope, sometimes dipped in tar, into any crack or space to seal them up.

Fresh food and water was enjoyed and as had been planned, wine and meat were bought, although Flinders complained at the cost. The East India Company, interested in the exploration, had advanced £600 for provisions, but this had to be used carefully as it was intended for the whole voyage, a further £600 to be paid on its successful completion.

> The prices charged for our ships supplies were as follows — Water sent on board in shore boats at 7/6 per ton. Wine of a tolerable quality at 5/8 per gal. besides charges for the casks and boat hire. Fresh beef at 10d. per lb. Which was tolerably good meat, but was ill dressed. The Best Madeira was £42 per pipe. We got our clothes moderately well washed at an extravagant price.

Leaving Madeira, they sailed south, well away from the coast of Africa and on the 7th September crossed the Equator. Seaman Smith describes "the usuil Seremony of Neptune and his Attendance hailing the Ship and coming on Board. The greatest part of the Officers and Men was shaved, not having cross'd the line before." There was an extra issue of grog and Flinders wrote: "The seamen were furnished with the means and permission to conclude the day with merriment."

Ever concerned about the health of his crew, Flinders allowed occasional times of what he called merriments. On fine evenings fifes and drums were played on the forecastle, where there was sometimes dancing and, as he put it, "he did not discourage other playful amusements which might occasionally be more to the taste of the sailors". Following the example of James Cook, he ruled that on every fine day the deck below and the cockpit should be washed, sprinkled with vinegar and aired; on wet days they were swept and aired. To prevent chill there was no sleeping on deck, or lying down in wet clothes, and about once a fortnight on a fine day all beds and contents of chests and baggage had to be brought on deck and aired in the sunshine. On Sundays and Thursdays every man had to appear washed, clean shaven and wearing clean clothes, provision of water being made for this and for the proper cleaning of cooking utensils.

The diet was monotonous, but was varied as much as possible. Sailing towards the Cape of Good Hope, Flinders wrote on 3rd September that he wanted to stay there for as short a time as possible and it was necessary, therefore, to keep the men in good health so that a prolonged stay would not be necessary. After consulting Bell, the surgeon, it was agreed that oatmeal should be boiled for breakfast on four mornings a week and boiled rice on the other days. Boiled peas were to be eaten for dinner on four days and on the other days each man was to have portable soup with barley, onions and pepper and anything else added. Thus they would have two hot meals and in addition they would be served with meat. Lime juice and sugar were to be issued for as long as possible, after which sauerkraut would be served.

On examining the stores it was found that the whole of the barley was spoiled. When the portable soup was boiled up by itself, the men would not touch it, so it was ordered that each man should be served two ounces of it, mixed with biscuits, three times a week and those who took it and wasted it were threatened with punishment.

On arrival in South Africa in mid October, the ship had to be re-caulked again. The crew were in excellent health and were able to have fresh food and the luxury of oranges. The only casualty was poor John Crosley, the astronomer, who was taken ill again and it was thought that it was impossible for him to continue. Flinders himself, together with his brother Samuel, who had acted as an assistant to John Crosley, took over the astronomer's duties. This did throw extra work on Flinders as although his brother was perfectly competent, he was inclined to be idle and irresponsible, and he was only about nineteen. Two seamen had not proved satisfactory and Vice Admiral Sir Roger Curtis, the Commander-in-Chief at the Cape, arranged for them to be exchanged for two others from ships stationed there.

After eighteen days they were off again to some disappointment on the part of the botanists who had been collecting plants from Table Mountain. The next stage of the voyage was uneventful: less water was seeping in and there was time for scientific observations and experiments. Up to this time ships' compasses gave unreliable measurements because they were affected by any piece of iron nearby or in the body of the ship. Ever since the first day out from England Flinders had carried out observations on the variations of the compass and also the effect of different winds on the mercury of the barometer, and observations are recorded in detail throughout his writings. These were problems that affected all ships and in time the solving of them was one of his great achievements.

The coast of New Holland, as it was known then, was seen at Cape Leeuwin on 6th December 1801 and careful observations began. It had been sighted by three previous expeditions, namely those commanded by the Dutchman Pieter Nuyts in 1627, by the Englishman George Vancouver in 1791 and by the Frenchman, Chevalier Joseph-Antoine D'Entrecasteaux in 1792. All had continued further, but had had to turn back.

Heading south in fine weather the *Investigator* passed what is described in the log as the smooth brown cliffs of Cape Howe and by the late evening of 8th December, with the light falling, Flinders put his faith in Vancouver's chart and his own seamanship and entered King George's Sound, (the furthest point reached by Vancouver) coming to anchor between Seal Island and Bald Head at 11.30 p.m. in 8 fathoms of water with a sandy bottom. A sense of achievement must have been felt by all on board. They had arrived safely on the coast of this great continent largely unknown to Europeans, and two thousand miles of coast lay eastward waiting to be charted.

Admiralty orders were to proceed straight to Port Jackson where the crew could have some respite and fresh supplies collected, and then to return to the southern coast to make a complete examination. Had Ann been on board, Flinders would probably done this, having made arrangements for her to stay at Port Jackson as it was never his intention to have her present whilst the tedious and often dangerous work of exploration and charting was in progress. The Admiralty did permit the commander of an expedition to use his own judgment as to how the spirit of orders was carried out. To continue to Port Jackson and then wait there before returning to avoid the winter storms and likelihood of bad visibility, seemed to be a waste of time. With sufficient supplies in the store, he determined to undertake the exploration and charting of this unknown coast as he went eastwards, and thus arrive at Port Jackson having achieved this just before the weather was likely to deteriorate.

* * *

Meanwhile, in St George's Sound no time was wasted. In the morning the "scientific gentlemen", that is the naturalists, botanists and artists, were sent in a boat to Bald Head, so called by Vancouver because of it barren shape. They were probably only too ready to start their work of searching and recording, as they had travelled as passengers, which at times must have been tedious: although Brown would have been spending time making a catalogue of specimen plants collected during the short stays at Madeira and the Cape and Bauer making drawings ready to be worked up later. When in Vienna he had learnt to use a colour chart, making his sketches with numbers and as the charts contained about 1,000 different shades, he could paint accurately at a later date. Visiting Oyster Island they were able to bring back plenty of shell fish for the whole crew. This would have been welcome fresh food, but would not have been the luxury with which oysters are regarded today. Up to mid-Victorian times oysters, together with salmon, were a cheap food obtainable from the Thames and it was laid down that apprentices should not be served such food more than two or three times a week. The convicts at Port Arthur in Van Diemen's Land were to be fed very largely on salmon and oysters, although they were also allowed to go out to shoot kangaroo for meat.

Flinders and Thistle, the Master, set off to Princess Royal Harbour to find what he called "a convenient place to wood, water and re-fit the ship", calling at Seal Island to look for a bottle and parchment that Vancouver was known to have left there, but they found no trace of it. They had some difficulty in finding a suitable anchorage and a strong wind got up which caused them to get drenched with spray, but by the 12th December they were able to take the ship into Princess Royal Harbour.

They were to stay for about two weeks, which gave them a break from the rolling seas and the creaking sounds of the ship. The land was explored, scientific instruments landed and checked, work done on the sails and rigging, and more re-caulking was necessary. Some went fishing and water and firewood were taken aboard: a marquee and a bell tent were put up for use as an observatory and other tents were brought ashore to pitch near the water supply.

A party of local inhabitants was met and although shy they accepted a gift of a bird which had just been shot and also a pocket handkerchief. Two days later they came to the tents and were given a number of presents. More native inhabitants came to look at them and were friendly and curious, although on one occasion Seaman Smith records that they threw pieces of wood at the sailors because they would not part with a tool they were using "but Orders being so Humane towards the Natives that we must put up with every thing but heaving Spears". He adds that the natives rubbed their skins against them and were surprised that the white colour did not come off, and described two of them running into the bushes with such activity "that would pawl any European to Exibit, without clothing".

Flinders tried speaking in the Port Jackson accent, but not surprisingly this was not understood, so sign language was used. He recounts:

> Our friends, the natives, continued to visit us: and an old man with several others being at the tents this morning, I ordered the party of marines on shore to be exercised in their presence. The red coats and white crossed belts were greatly admired, having some resemblance to their

own manner of ornamenting themselves; and the drum, but particularly the fife, excited their astonishment; but when they saw these beautiful red and white men with their bright muskets drawn up in a line, they absolutely screamed with delight; nor were their wild gestures to be silenced but by commencing the exercise, to which they paid the most earnest and silent attention. Several of them moved their hands, involuntarily, according to the motions and the old man placed himself at the end of the rank, with a short staff in his hand, which he shouldered, presented, grounded, as did the marines with their muskets without I believe knowing what he did. Before firing, the Indians were made acquainted with what was going to take place; so that the volleys did not excite much terror.

The botanists quickly collected a number of plants and Westall drew a detailed picture of King George's Sound before they sailed on towards the Great Bight as Flinders was to name this stretch of coast. With meticulous care every feature was recorded as he was determined that after he had made his charts and reports there would be no need for anyone else to follow him to revise. This was not the case with earlier explorers in other waters, men such as Cook or Tasman who, unlike Flinders, did not go back to the point where they were when night fell, and therefore there were often gaps and inaccuracies in their more sketchy charts. The artists and naturalists went ashore whenever possible to draw and to collect specimens. The heat was intense and on one day Bauer suffered from sunstroke.

On 7th January the record reads:

> Tacking to weather the Doubtful Islands ....Light winds and fine weather. Cleaned below and aired the stores. Served sour krout and vinegar to the ships company and sweet wort also.

By the 10th January they were passing the D'Entrecausteaux Islands, and the journal records the day in some detail.

Wanting to get a better knowledge of the archipelago than a run through would give, and to allow the accuracy of the time keepers to be checked, Flinders agreed to the request of the naturalists to stay a day or two. Early in the morning a party went ashore, and he followed in another boat. After taking some measurements for altitude he climbed a hill to take bearings of what was in sight, but the islands and reefs were so numerous that he records it was very perplexing and the haziness of the weather prevented seeing more than eight or nine miles; however he did measure altitudes and took six sets of lunar observations. On top of the hill he had found the botanizing party "regaling on palm nuts, which were rather abundant there but the greater part of those that eat them were ill afterwards sick."

On coming down the hill they found a large nest in a low tree, apparently from the look of the feathers belonging to the same kind of birds they had seen in King George's Sound. It was a recent nest, with bits of bone and hair lying below "similar to what owls throw up after swallowing mice", but in this case it was penguin feathers, seal's fur and the skin and head of a large lizard. The nest, which was quite flat, measured 3 or 3½ feet in diameter. On looking along the coastline he mentions rocks and reefs "so tremendous obnoxious to a seaman's eye". The interior of the country, looked little better, not covered with much vegetation and without a blade of grass fit for cattle to eat or a square yard of soil worth cultivating.

On the 12th January the journal records:

> At noon I landed on the east side of the bay, and observed the supplement of the suns altitude, which

gave latitude 33°.59'49"So. I observed, that the granite of the islands which form the east side of this bay, appears to be in a state of decomposition. Its surface is scaling off in pieces of from the smallest size to such as are masses of the size bigness of a ships hull; these last form large caves in some places, in one of which I found two swallows nests, but did not observe any thing remarkable in their structure.

In the evening the master returned. He had found a small bay of a sufficient size to receive one ship and keep her in the greatest security. She would lie in the west corner, with a bower anchor towards the entrance and a stream anchor on her quarter, and with a hawser on shore from the starboard bow and quarter; so secured she would lie almost near enough to the shore, in from 3 to 5 fms. Water, as to lay a stage to the shore. The landing is very smooth with all winds and there is a sufficient quantity of small wood to supply more than one ship with fuel. A beach surrounds the bay, and at the back of it, at a less distance than a hundred yards, is a lagoon of near a mile in circumference, containing very good water....

From this snug little bay, the master proceeded to the westward, and from the top of an island marked p in the chart, took some angles, and gave me the form of the coast for five or six miles in that direction he likewise met with geese and seals amongst the islands, but he was not prepared for the former.

[Tuesday] — 12th. Light breezes and cloudy: afterwards fine weather. Sent a boat to kill seals, and the master to examine the coast and the islands to the eastwards. People employed occasionally.

A shark, (one of three seen of the same size) caught alongside this morning whose dimensions were as follows

	Ft.
Extreme length	12.3
Greatest girth	8.0
Back fin from nose	4.8
Outer part of jaw bones (forming the Diameter of his mouth)	1.10
Length of each breast fin	2.4
Breadth of (do.)	1.5
Height of his back fin	1.4

The following day the 1st Lieutenant and the Master took the boat to an island some seven miles off the coast where they reported there were a number of kangaroos and some seals whose fur was red and very poor, but there was no sign of human habitation. Brown made an expedition to the highest peak in the neighbourhood where he found the top appeared to have been excavated, with a large piece "lying upon the top of the mount like a cap to it. He represents the country as miserably barren". Flinders himself spent the day checking altitudes and checking the time-keepers until the evening when he records fresh gales and hazy weather.

By the 20th they were off Nuyt's Land where the windings of the coast made it difficult as they projected so little that long before the ship came up to them they were lost among the uniform range and little remained to be noted. This is described as "a considerable inconvenience to the survey", although at one point the cliff was white as though rocks had only recently fallen off.

A few days later the swell from the south caused the *Investigator* to labour and as a result the old leaks opened again and she was making one or two inches of water an hour. The wind prevented them from making progress and it is recorded rather ruefully that "if we could have supposed the wind would have remained at E.6.N. all the morning it would have been advantageous to have been in with the shore at 7 or 8 o'clock".

By noon on the 28th January they were abreast of a cliff from which the land turned north east and into the "great gulph of New Holland". It was hazy, so difficult to see far inland, but the coastline had a coat of shabby vegetation with "sand peeping thro' in ten thousand places". The journal continues to record the bleakness of the land, but from fires seen in the distance it seemed that there were a few people living there.

On 4th February 1802 he reported:

> The small bay in the Isle of St Francis, which I call Petrel Bay, affords excellent shelter for two or three ships; but no fresh water, not even to rince our mouths, could be found at this time and a few scattered bushes were the nearest approach to wood upon the island. Petrels, penguins and a few hair seals may be procured, and probably some geese in season.

The winds, the position of the ship and the astronomical calculations are all recorded in the journal and there is a paragraph explaining how at different times Flinders found disagreements between measurements taken on different tacks which he thought might arise from the two guns upon the quarter deck which were placed opposite the binnacle. Therefore, he had them removed and taken down to the hold, writing that his opinion had sometimes fluctuated between the guns or magnetism from the rocks of the neighbouring land being the cause of these differences. On another occasion Flinders had the seamen searching for needles in case one should have been dropped on the deck and so affected the compass.

As they continued Flinders named many of the coastal

features — names which are still used today. Some are called after members of his crew, others after distinguished men such as Earl Spencer and Sir Joseph Banks. He never named a place after himself and Flinders Island, in the Investigator Group, is named after his brother Samuel. Other places bearing his name have been so called in modern times. Occasionally places were named because of incidents, such as Lucky Bay, where they had been able to take shelter and stay for four days, or, sadly, Cape Catastrophe where John Thistle and a midshipman called William Taylor and six sailors lost their lives when attempting to bring back fresh water.

It had been the intention to get under weigh by noon on 22nd February, but as there were considerable differences in the longitudes given by the time keepers on board, they stayed to get measurements on shore. At seven o'clock in the evening Thistle took a boat with the seven men to search for fresh water, and it was seen returning, but was suddenly lost from sight. Fowler, the First Lieutenant, was sent in another boat to see what had happened. At 9.30 a gun was fired as a signal to return, which he did in about half an hour. Fowler had seen no sight of Thistle's boat but reported that his own boat had been nearly swamped by getting into a rippling of the tide where the water broke sometimes suddenly.

At first light next morning a thorough search was started by two parties walking along the shore in opposite directions, a look-out man climbing up a headland and a cutter sent along the shore. The cutter returned towing the wreck of Thistle's boat which appeared to have been dashed against rocks and later an oar was found, but there was no sign of the men. Ironically, there was what is described as an ineffectual supply of water inland.

The loss of John Thistle was a serious blow to Flinders and he wrote later in *"A Voyage to Terra Australis"*:

> Mr Thistle was truly a valuable man, as a seaman, an officer, and a good member of society. I had known him, and we had mainly sailed together from 1794. He had been with Mr Bass in his perilous expedition in the whale boat, and with me around Van Diemen's Land, and in the succeeding expeditions, to Glasshouse and Hervey's Bays. From his merit and prudent conduct he was promoted from before the mast to be a midshipman and afterwards a Master in His Majesty's Service. His zeal for discovery had induced him to join the *Investigator* when at Spithead and ready to sail, although he had returned to England only two weeks before, after an absence of six years. His loss was severely felt by me; and he was lamented by all on board, more especially by his messmates, who knew more intimately the goodness and stability of his disposition. I caused an inscription to be engraved upon a sheet of copper, and set up on a stout post at the head of the cove which I named Memory Cove; and to further commemorate our loss, I gave to each of these six islands nearest to Cape Catastrophe the name of one of the seamen: Thistle's and Taylor's Islands having already been named.

> H.M.S. Investigator, M. Flinders Comr.
> Anchored here Feb.22. 1802
> Mr. John Thistle, the Master.
> Mr. William Taylor, Midn. And
> six of the crew were most unfortunately
> drowned near this place from being upset
> in a boat. The wreck of the boat was found,
> but their bodies were not recovered.

> Nautici, cavete!

The whole crew was affected but after four days searching the voyage had to go on. It was with a heavy heart that Flinders had to appoint Thomas Evans to act in the capacity of Master until further orders.

They were about to round the headland into Spencer's Gulf. There was much speculation from the way the tides ran and the fact that the coast ran sharply north but no coast could be seen to the east, that this was the southerly point of the strait which was thought might run down from the Gulf of Carpentaria and so divide New Holland from New South Wales. This was of immense interest and there was considerable talk about it, which must have helped to take their minds off the recent disastrous days.

> Large rivers, deep inlets and passages into the Gulf of Carpentaria, were terms frequently used in our conversations of this evening, and the prospect of making an interesting discovery seemed to infuse new life and vigour into every man on the ship.

The exploration of the gulf began and it was then that Flinders continued naming various features after the towns and villages in Lincolnshire, having named Sleaford Bay previously. One group of islands was called after Sir Joseph Banks, whilst a slightly larger one was called Revesby, where Banks lived in Lincolnshire.

> In the morning, we sailed for the newly discovered inlet and at two o'clock passed around the projection, which formed the south side of the entrance to the new opening and is named Cape Donington. In steering south westward we left an island four miles long, named Boston Island, on the starboard hand, and passed two islets on the other side, called Bicker Isles which lie off Surfleet Point. The hill which had been seen from Thistle's Island when seen to the north or south assumes a conical form. I named it Stamford Hill. Between Cape Donington, at the entrance, and

Surfleet Point, was a large cove with a sandy beach at the head capable of sheltering a fleet of ships: this was named Spalding Cove.

On the north side of the port; higher up, was a projecting piece of land with an island lying off it nearly one mile in length. This island was named Grantham Island.

The eastern entrance to the port between Boston Island and Cape Donington is one mile and a half wide; the western entrance between the island and what was called Kirton Point is larger. From Kirton Point northward the shore curves back forming a bay named Boston Bay.

The port which formed the most interesting part of these Discoveries I named Port Lincoln, in honour of my native province.

The *Investigator* spent five days at Port Lincoln, during which time a great deal of scientific work was carried out both by the scientists and Flinders himself and on the last day they witnessed a solar eclipse.

It was to Port Lincoln that Sir John Franklin (as he had become) was to return on 12th January 1841, when he was Lieutenant Governor of Van Diemen's Land, to lay a stone to the memory of "Matthew Flinders, R.N., Commander of H.M.S. Investigator, the discoverer of the country now called South Australia".

Soon the coastline opposite was seen, indicating that it was a wide bay, and on 10th March Flinders, accompanied by Surgeon Bell took a rowing boat, rowing along the shore and sleeping overnight in the boat. Setting off again at first light they found that by ten o'clock the oars were touching mud and it was obvious that there was no strait running northwards, so they returned to the *Investigator* and continued charting the coastline, down the eastern side of the Gulf.

Careful progress continued southwards again, until they

rounded Cape Spencer on 20th March, and on towards the northern coastline of what was to be named Kangaroo Island, so called because of the very large number of them to be seen there. Initially, unsure whether or not it was a lengthy promontory, it was described as a large Uncertain Island. Nearing the coast many dark rocks were thought to be seen: one or two members of the crew said that some of them jumped about which caused much hilarity until it was seen that these shapes were kangaroos. After months of eating salt pork although relieved occasionally by fresh fish and meat it is not surprising that a substantial number were shot. Although Flinders obviously did not care for this, saying that the poor creatures stood up to be shot between the eyes, he recorded that feasts of fresh meat were consumed. They did not stay long, but crossed Investigator's Strait and into the Gulf of St. Vincent, sighting Mount Lofty and the area where Adelaide now stands on 28th March. Further north Flinders again realized there was no strait dividing New South Wales from New Holland and so turned back down the other side of the gulf to head for Kangaroo Island, where they stayed for five days.

In addition to careful details of the position, the winds, the depth of water and the daily work of the ship and the food served, the journal describes the scenery and rock formations and records seeing smoke from fires on the mainland which indicated that the country was inhabited, and it also records hearing the howling of dogs. The visits on shore which Brown, Bauer and Westall made to collect specimens, climb some hills and to make drawings were also noted.

Shooting parties went ashore to get plentiful supplies of fresh meat: others collected wood for the stove and fresh water, whilst the scientists set out to collect plants. Flinders spent time on the island, firstly to make observations for ascertaining the rate of the time keepers and their error from Greenwich mean time but also to explore the land in the fine weather they were enjoying. He thought the country had a pleasant appearance but was not very fertile. He did record in some detail his visit to two small islands in what is called Pelican Lagoon because it appeared to be a breeding ground for them.

> These birds were in great numbers, and many of them were too young to fly. From the number quantity of skeletons and scattered bones upon one of the islands, I infer that the pelicans also end their days there ....
> not only commence their being here, but that they have selected this retreat for the closing scene of their existence; here, at a distance from man, the great disturber of all the vital principal that animated them, can quietly depart, without interruption, and perhaps without a pang.

Flocks of emu, seals and black swan were seen. Trunks and branches of trees lay about and it seemed that they had not fallen down because of age or a gale as there were marks of fire on them. They had seen fallen trees in much the same state on Thistle's Island and Boston Island and concluded that they had been struck by lightning some ten or twenty years before. Kangaroo Island was uninhabited so the marks could not have been caused by natives' fires but they may well have caught fire naturally in a very hot summer. Mount Lofty could be seen to the north, and today one can drive up there from Adelaide to the observation post and see the reverse of the view seen by Flinders.

* * *

It was by then autumn, and the ship's provisions were beginning to run low, so it was decided to leave careful charting of Kangaroo Island, with the intention of returning in the future. The wind and tide were against them and slow progress was being made when the lookout man shouted that there was a white rock ahead. Quickly it became clear that it was no rock but the sails of a ship. This was not on any trade route, for it was new uncharted territory but Flinders knew before he left home that there was a French expedition heading for Australian waters which should be carrying a passport and that it was likely to be captained by Nicolas Baudin. As he could not be sure and in case by some chance it was a French warship, he ordered that the *Investigator* be "cleared for action in case of being attacked". As the ship approached, the Union Jack (which had been adopted in 1801 just before the departure from England) was hoisted and the French tricolour was seen to be run up "and afterwards an English Jack forward, as we did a white flag". It was indeed Baudin in the ship *Le Géographe*.

The second ship in the French expedition, *Le Naturaliste* had separated near the eastern entrance to the Bass Strait, and Baudin had first thought they were meeting up again and it was not until the *Investigator's* flag was seen that he realised that this was not so. Baudin had come through the Bass Strait and sailed along the coast in very good weather, but he had missed a number of landmarks.

At 5.30 in the evening *Le Géographe* passed close to the *Investigator* in the following wind and Flinders was able to shout out "Are you Captain Baudin?" and the answer came back that he was. Flinders answered that he was very glad to meet him and again Baudin replied, although he did not know Flinders' name. Flinders was still cautious and veered round to keep the guns trained on *Le Géographe* in case the flag of truce should be a deception, but on being satisfied that all was well he brought the ship round again. A boat was lowered and Flinders went on board the

French ship, accompanied by Robert Brown, who spoke fluent French, whereas Flinders knew none, and Baudin took them both to his cabin.

The accounts written by Baudin and Flinders differ in detail, Baudin stating that Flinders and he were alone, Flinders making it clear that Brown was present: Baudin may have thought that as Brown was merely the interpreter he could ignore him. Baudin considered he spoke English well enough to be understood, although in fact his command of the language was poor. Flinders produced his passport from the French government which Baudin laid on the table without looking at it, but he produced his own from the British government.

Flinders explained he was heading for Port Jackson, charting the unknown coast as he went. Baudin had left France before the *Investigator*'s departure from England. He had kept close to the African coast, so failing to make use of favourable trade winds and had made a very slow passage to Mauritius, much to the displeasure of his officers. He then spent about five weeks there, where he left six of his scientists, before sailing down the western coast of what was still known as New Holland to Port Leeuwin which he reached at the end of May 1801. It was then getting wintry, so he turned north towards Timor, where six of the crew died of dysentery, including his botanist. Held up for a time by bad weather, Baudin then continued in a leisurely manner by a known and lengthy route southwards and round Van Diemen's Land. For the second time his accompanying ship became separated in poor weather. Time had been spent on the eastern and southern coast of Van Diemen's Land where he had lost his geographers and the crew of a boat and he had then come through the Bass Strait sailing westwards. He missed the sizeable island, already named King Island, saying he doubted its existence and had missed the harbour that was to become Port Philip. (Louis de Freycinet and François Péron, who wrote up the account of *Le Géographe's* voyage, were to say that this harbour was sighted, but from the position from which it was claimed to have been seen, this was impossible.)

Baudin had an English chart of the Bass Strait which had been published in 1800 but of which he was critical saying that although the south side was accurate (it was made by Flinders) the northerly side was not. Flinders pointed to a note explaining that the chart of the northern side was made up from the fairly rough charts made by George Bass when in the whale boat, and when he only had the very simplest equipment which could not accurately measure latitude and longitude and which Flinders had thought to be faulty. He added that the chart had been amended and as he had a copy he would bring one over next morning if Baudin would be willing to stay alongside overnight. He happily agreed. Baudin was to state that he knew who Flinders was from the beginning, but Flinders did not think he did until the end of the second meeting. Baudin asked if a lookout could be kept for *Le Naturaliste* which Flinders agreed to do. He wrote "On my asking the name of the commander of *Le Naturaliste*, he besought himself to ask mine; and finding it to be the same as the author of the chart he had been criticizing, expressed not a little surprise, but had the politeness to congratulate himself on meeting me". They parted very amicably at 8.30 in the morning of the 9th April but when back aboard the *Investigator* Flinders was heard to remark that he thought Baudin's charts were "rather below mediocrity".

Having seen the sorry state of the French crew, many of them obviously suffering from scurvy, Flinders invited Baudin back to Port Jackson but suggested he first visit nearby Kangaroo Island where they might be able to get a brief respite and gave him information about safe anchorages. Baudin took his advice and sailed on to the southern coast of the island where he spent just over three weeks. His hard pressed crew would have been able to get some fresh meat, water and perhaps some fish but they had little relief from work as a survey of the southern coast of the island was carried out. With scurvy seriously affecting his men he had to abandon the survey on the 8th May, hoping to return after he had rested at Port Jackson.

Naming it Encounter Bay to commemorate this extraordinary and historic meeting, Flinders sailed on eastwards but, like Baudin, he was to miss the mouth of the Murray river behind its huge sandbanks. We shall never know what his inner thoughts were. Baudin's area of original discovery was only a hundred and fifty miles but Flinders must have felt a tinge of disappointment that he was not to be the original discoverer from King George's Sound to Western Port, where Bass had had to abandon his voyage in the whale boat. Nevertheless, he had defeated the object of the French expedition to claim to be the first on the southern coast.

What Flinders did not know was that Lieutenant Grant commanding the *Lady Nelson* had been on the coast as well. He had received his sailing orders in England in January 1800, and whilst at Cape Town a ship arrived from home with orders to proceed to the Bass Strait, using Flinders' charts, instead of taking a more southerly route and going round Van Diemen's Land to Port Jackson. He had sighted the Australian Coast at the point he named Cape Banks before sailing through the Bass Strait to Port Jackson.

Grant did not make a detailed survey, although he marked

and named prominent features along the shoreline, and as he was getting short of water and provisions he headed straight for Port Jackson, making what he called eye sketches of the coast. He was to make another excursion as far as Western Port, where he was confined by bad weather and provisions again running low he went back to Port Jackson disappointed and then returned to England. It seems a little hard that Governor King should write to him "I should have been glad if your abilities as a surveyor, or being able to determine the longitude of the different places you might visit, was any ways equal to your ability as an officer and a seaman", but years later Flinders writing his *"Voyage to Terra Australis"* compared his own rough charts with Grant's and found that the longitudes for places Grant had named were often very inaccurate. Nevertheless, Flinders gave Grant the credit for being the first on that stretch of the coast.

The *Investigator* ran into severe weather after leaving Encounter Bay and detailed survey was difficult. On the night of the 20th April Flinders described the very great danger they were in as they tossed about in the darkness, and he feared they might hit an island or go down, but as the weather moderated he guessed they were to windward of a large island which proved to be King Island, the southern coast of which had been visited by Captain Reid in a seal hunting ship in 1799. Flinders did not know that it had also been visited by Captain John Black in January 1801, who had named it King Island. It was to be Flinders' role to link together their findings to make accurate charts.

As there was a good anchorage Flinders, Robert Brown and others went ashore that evening and again early the next morning and collected a large number of plants, some of them ones they had not seen before and they wrote a report about the vegetation. Nearing the end of the voyage there was concern that some of the provisions were getting low, but judging from the height of the barometer it seemed that the weather would remain fine and Flinders determined to return to the mainland coast. The wind was such that the *Investigator* had to continue the survey rather further east than intended, and so approach what was to prove to be the entrance to Port Philip — that great harbour on whose shore the city of Melbourne was to be built, largely because of the good reports that Flinders made about the surrounding country. Beyond a rocky point, a small opening was seen with water breaking across. Coming nearer a large extent of water spread out beyond and in spite of the narrow entrance and what he called the "ripplings like breakers", he decided to take the ship in with every man ready to tack at a moment's notice.

> The soundings were very irregular the depth diminished from ten fathoms to three; and before the ship could come round, the flood tide set her upon a mud bank and she stuck fast. A boat was lowered down to sound; and finding deep water lie to the north west, a kedge anchor was carried out, and having got the ship's head in that direction, the sails were filled, and she drew off into six and ten fathoms; and it being dark, we came to an anchor.

Seaman Smith had something to say about this.

> On the 28th we came to an Anchor in A Bay of A Very large size. Thinking there was A good Channel in A passage through, we got Aground; but by good Manadgement we got of without Damadge. Here we caught A Shirk which Measured 10 Feet 9 Inches in Length; in girt very large.

It seems he was more interested in the size of the shark

than in what must have been an alarming time in getting the ship off the shoal.

What Flinders also did not know was that Lieutenant John Murray who succeeded James Grant in command of the *Lady Nelson* had also been on this coast and had actually entered the harbour on 14th February 1802, calling it a noble sheet of water. He was much more cautious than Flinders and had sent the Master in a boat to find a channel deep enough to take in the *Lady Nelson*, a ship far smaller than the *Investigator*. He made a simple plan of Port Philip and wrote some interesting descriptions, at one point saying that its beauty fell nothing short of Greenwich Park and he named Arthur's Seat as it reminded him of the mountain at Edinburgh.

Knowing nothing of all this Flinders spent six days making a meticulous examination. At first he thought that he might have entered Western Port but was puzzled that this narrow and dangerous entrance was quite unlike that described by George Bass. As light dawned on the next morning, 27th April, he saw that this expansive bay was very different. After making observations for latitude, Flinders with a group of others including John Franklin, William Westall and Robert Brown, took a boat to the shore and then climbed Arthur's Seat where they were amazed at the size of the bay below them. Walking along the ridge and taking bearings they realised that they could see Western Port to the east. Brown wasted no time and made a large quantity of notes about plants, trees, birds and animals and the type of soil before they came back to the shore and had a picnic of oysters before returning to the ship. Ferdinand Bauer, Peter Good and John Allen had landed separately and made a list of plants they saw. Clearly, it was a good day which they enjoyed after their experiences of the storms. Those left on board had to

Matthew Flinders' birthplace, Donington, Lincolnshire. Artist's impression by Jane Body based on a photograph taken before the house was demolished in 1908.

Model of H.M.S. Investigator

Government House, Sydney, Drawing by William Westall 1802.
National Library of Australia, Canberra

Sailors on Kangaroo Island
Sketch by William Westall 1802.
National Library of Australia, Canberra.

spend the day "drying the sails which had gotten wet in the sail room from leaks during the last gale".

The following day the ship sailed round the bay, but with a very light wind progress was too slow, so Lieutenant Fowler had to take the ship back to the anchorage which he did with some difficulty, whilst Flinders with a couple of seamen took a boat, staying out four days supplementing the ship's rations with the duck they shot, and making a very accurate survey of a substantial area. They met some of the native inhabitants, exchanged presents and shared a meal with them. Rowing northwards, he climbed the mountain he had seen from the entrance to the bay, and at the point he named Station Peak he left a scroll of paper under a pile of stones to record his climb. A bronze plate was put up there many years later. He wrote that he got back to the tent by the shore very tired, having walked more than twenty miles without finding a drop of water. Taking soundings on the way back to the ship he returned the next day — a day later than he had anticipated which must had caused some anxiety. The scientists and Peter Good and others had all taken other boats and spent their days on the shore to make notes and drawings.

There was no trouble in navigating the passage out to the sea but Flinders in his report did stress its dangers and on his chart the words "strong tide ripplings" appear. He wrote an instruction which read:-

> It will always be desirable for vessels to get sight of this cape (Cape Schanck) before being run far into the great bight for Port Philip, and if the wind blows strong from the southward it will be unsafe to run without having seen it.

From five miles out William Westall drew a picture, which was attached to the chart to help those who in future might enter what Flinders described as an extensive but obscure port.

In the last few days of the voyage Flinders made observations of the coast which Bass had seen and made the corrections that were necessary because of Bass's damaged quadrant, and finally Sydney Heads were seen. An attempt to get into the familiar harbour at night was made, but the wind made it impossible. On the 10th May, with a pilot on board they were at the mouth of Sydney Cove, the cutter was lowered and Flinders landed to call upon the Governor, and at dawn on 11th May the *Investigator* anchored near Bennelong Point where Sydney's great Opera House stands today. The splash must have made all those on board proud of their achievement. Not only had they accomplished a voyage that was to affect the course of history, but except for the tragic accident at Cape Catastrophe most of them had arrived in astonishingly good health without a sign of scurvy or other diseases which normally afflicted men on long voyages. One marine had to be discharged and was sent back to England as he appeared to be contracting tuberculosis and three others were described as unwell, but nevertheless every member of the crew was on deck to work the ship into the harbour.

6

Port Jackson

The two months stay at Port Jackson was intended to be a time of preparation for the next stage — the continuation northwards and the careful charting of the northern coast. There was no holiday or time off and the journal for the following day records the weather, as was usual, when there were light and moderate breezes alternatively and rain at times.

Two bell tents and what was called a markee were put up on the eastern point of the cove, so that the observatory and instruments could be sent ashore for examination, these tents being guarded by four marines. They began to land empty casks so that they could be checked and repaired by the cooper: some of the rigging was bad and so was unrove and sent ashore for inspection and the boatswain's stores had to be inspected.

Flinders had found the barricading on the quarter deck, which had been put on at Chatham, was an obstruction to surveying and he had considered it a detriment to the ship's sailing. A letter was written to the Governor[1], who was the senior naval officer, to ask if it might be removed. He ordered a survey to be made by the carpenters employed at Port Jackson, together with those from the *Lady Nelson* and the *Investigator* to see if this could be done without causing damage, following which an order was given to

---

[1] Philip Gidley King became Governor in April 1800, replacing John Hunter

remove it without delay, and four convicts were sent to help with the work.

The *Investigator* had to be extensively overhauled, her timbers checked, her sails taken down and spread on the shore to be examined for weaknesses and the necessary repairs. A new eight oared boat, costing £30, was built to replace the one lost at Cape Catastrophe and very importantly the planthouse had to be placed on the deck. This complicated structure, brought out from England in what today we might call kit form, had to be assembled on deck and very carefully bolted into the right position so that there would be sufficient space to get round it on an already congested deck and not impede seriously the working of the ship or upset the balance. It was found to be too large and had to be reduced in size by one third. This work was done by convicts aboard the old ship *Supply*, now a hulk in the harbour.

Samuel Smith described the scene:

> Here we unrigg'd and rigg'd our ship, likewise painted
> her and received a stock of provisions .... The town of
> Sidney is Built in the form of A Crescent, the streets in
> a regulour form, altho not paved, the Houses are Built
> in regulour lines, and must not exceed the limits of the
> line on the proper run of the streets. The Buildings
> are covered with Shingles made of shee oak in the form
> of A slate which are used in England.

With instant communication today it may be difficult to realize the problems of keeping in touch with home two hundred years ago. Some of those who found themselves in far-flung places may not have wished to do so, and probably many of those who arrived in Australia as convicts could not read or write and thus were completely cut off. The settlers, soldiers, sailors and government employees only had a hope that letters would arrive, although they would take at least six months and another six months or more would pass before any reply could reach home. Even in the 1930s mail was slow and letters to Australia from England took five weeks or more going by sea. It was not until the airmail service began to be established that letters took a mere ten days.

Knowing that he and Ann had to rely on the Admiralty's Naval Transport Office and the chance of a ship being available, Flinders was nevertheless disappointed that there was no letter from her. He wrote to her to say that he was safe and well and had done everything that he could be expected to do. "How highly I should value such short information reciprocated from thee! But also my dearest love, I am in the dark concerning thee, I know not what to fear or what to hope". He was especially saddened that Ann had not been allowed to travel with him as Mrs. King, the wife of the Governor, and Mrs. Paterson, the wife of the Deputy Governor, would have befriended her and become what he called her choicest friends.

There can have been very little social life in those early days in Sydney but the 4th June, the King's birthday, was celebrated with a dinner at Government House followed by a dance. Flinders wrote to Ann to describe the forthcoming occasion "at which 52 gentlemen and ladies will be present" and recalling a dance at Spilsby which they both must have attended as being preferable to what was to take place that night. The *Investigator* was dressed with colours and a royal salute fired and on 11th June a salute of seventeen guns was fired when the Governor came on board.

On arrival at Port Jackson, Flinders had found *Le Naturaliste* in the harbour and he at once called on Captain Hamelin who had been forced to take refuge because of the weather conditions and the ill-health of the crew, and found that the French had been received with generous hospitality. It was not until the 20th June that *Le Géographe* was seen in difficulties beyond the Heads and men from the *Investigator* went out to bring her in. On the 22nd June Baudin visited Flinders, who the following day returned his call. The French officers and men were in a dreadful condition, only twelve of them capable of duty (Baudin recorded only four) and they too were suffering from the ulcers and appalling pain caused by scurvy, and were too weak to bring the ship into the harbour by themselves. Immediately the Governor did everything he could to help. Some of the men were taken to the hospital, others treated in the tents put up on the shore below Government House near the tents used by the *Investigator's* crew, and the colony's surgeon did all he could. The French surgeon had done his best, but suffering himself he was revolted with the constant treatment of ulcers. Flinders wrote that it was "grievous to see the conditions to which officers and men were reduced by scurvy". The colony's food supplies were not sufficient to cope with the arrival of the two French ships in need of so much attention, and some of the breeding stock of cattle had to be killed in order to supply fresh meat, and everyone else had to have their rations cut. Later Flinders complained that except on the King's birthday his men were allowed very little fresh meat or fish during their stay at Port Jackson: the crew could not be spared from their work to go off on fishing expeditions. The continual diet of dried and salted meat may well have contributed to the deterioration in the health of the *Investigator's* crew on the next stage of the voyage, although the Governor once or twice a week supplied them with fresh vegetables from his own garden.

On long voyages, lasting eighteen months or two years, it was inevitable that there would be outbreaks of scurvy and dysentery, as every explorer knew. Cook's proud boast was that none of his men had died of scurvy, but nevertheless some of them did contract it simply because of the lack of fresh food, although for as long as possible there was an issue of limes or lemons. Cook's ship the *Endeavour* called at Princes Island in the Indian Ocean on the way home for the purpose of getting fruit and fresh water, but this was badly infected and thirty men died from dysentery, including Sir Joseph Banks' two artists and his secretary, before the Cape of Good Hope was reached.

However it has to be said that Nicolas Baudin must take the blame for the sorry state of his crew. He was above all interested in scientific discovery and not in the leadership needed for voyages such as these. He had served in the French Merchant Navy, but during the Revolution he had gone to Austria and then travelled to both India and the West Indies, amassing a collection of natural species which he displayed in the Natural History Museum in Vienna. When war was declared between France and Austria in 1796 he took his collection to Paris where it came to the attention of Napoleon who in 1800 asked him to sail to the southern seas for the purpose of collecting more specimens, and with him sailed two scientists, François Péron and Lieutenant Louis de Freycinet. It was a very well financed expedition in which a number of other scientists took part, although six of them were left in Mauritius on the way.

By the time *Le Géographe* reached Encounter Bay eighteen months had passed since she left France and it was obvious that the health of the crew was deteriorating very seriously, being afflicted with both scurvy and dysentery, and Baudin, in spite of warnings from his officers was extraordinarily lackadaisical: Péron, naturalist that he was, complained that too much time was spent chasing butterflies. The visit to Kangaroo Island did mean that some water and fresh food could be had but the meat would have had to have been cooked as soon as shot and must have been stewed up for hours to make it edible. As a survey of the southern coast of the island was made, the ship's company cannot have had much chance of rest. On returning eastwards instead of going through the Bass Strait — and there was no reason not to do so — he chose to sail round van Diemen's Land, which added about another week to the voyage. He had little excuse for the lack of hygiene as his countryman La Pérouse had successfully put into practice the recommendations of James Cook, and these recommendations were available to Baudin. Not surprisingly morale was very low, his officers quarrelsome and discipline about hygiene difficult to enforce on a crew so weakened by illness.

The French ships were to stay at Port Jackson for several months, during which time a friendship developed between Baudin and Governor King who happily spoke good French. The free citizens of the colony went out of their way to make officers and men welcome. There was one occasion when Flinders gave dinner to Baudin, Hamelin, Péron and others and because the Deputy Governor, Colonel Paterson, was also a guest they were welcomed aboard with a salute of eleven guns. News had just been received that the French and British were no longer at war, but as Governor King had said previously, peace or war was to make no difference in the help to be given to those who were engaged in voyages of scientific discovery. As scientists, Péron and Freycinet were given the freedom to explore the surrounding land in order to collect specimen plants and they were provided with food and given any help they needed although Baudin himself did not encourage their expeditions. Sadly, later their reports were to show that they abused the privilege and the hospitality they received by spying out the land.

When the two French ships finally sailed on 17th November 1802 Baudin repeatedly expressed gratitude and he left with the Governor twelve copies of a letter to the governors of the French islands of Mauritius and Bourbon in which he spelled out the way they had been treated so liberally and asked that the respective governors should give the same kind of help to British ships in similar circumstances. Governor King was later to receive a Sèvres dinner service sent out from France as a personal gift.

No sooner had they gone than Colonel Paterson heard a rumour that some of the French officers had been boasting that they were going to found a French settlement in the eastern area of the Bass Strait. Although King had never doubted Baudin's assurance that the voyage was entirely of a scientific nature, nevertheless he sent Lieutenant Robbins after him, who finding him at King Island delivered a letter stating that this area had already been claimed by the British. Baudin wrote an official reply and also a personal one to the Governor denying any intention of making a claim for France. Young Robbins appears to have lost his head and landed his company of seventeen men to hoist the British flag alongside the tents put up on the shore by the French. Ordering the three Marines present to fire a volley and the rest of the men to cheer, he claimed formal possession of King Island for the British Crown. It seems that Robbins ran up the flag incorrectly as Baudin made a joke that he thought it was something used for straining water and the French thought it was rather entertaining. In spite of it all they remained on friendly terms until the French left King Island on the 27th December. Robbins stayed another three weeks, making a survey before, as ordered, he went on to Port Philip to complete the survey that Flinders had not the time to do. Flinders was to acknowledge the survey work of Robbins.

The *Investigator* had left Port Jackson long before, being ready to sail by the 21st July. Apart from preparations for the next part of the voyage detailed reports had to be written about the discoveries along the southern coast, and Flinders wrote a report to Sir Joseph Banks but the charts were not ready in time to be put on a ship then sailing for home. Banks was disappointed and wrote a letter expressing some annoyance and suggesting that duplicate charts should be made during the voyage. For a man who having sailed to Australia himself and so might have understood the conditions under which any charts were made at sea, this does show a strange lack of understanding. Flinders was not to receive Banks' letter until he was back at Port Jackson nearly a year later when he would have known that the charts were likely to be with Banks, and by then he had had so many cares on his mind that he may have regarded Banks' letter as a minor irritation.

Letters were written to Ann but when at last he did receive one from her it did not give him any cheer. We do not know exactly what she wrote because she was later to destroy all her own letters to her husband although she kept those he had written to her. However, it is clear from this letter that she was devastated. She had had to have an operation to save her eyesight because her excessive crying had caused her eye to be inflamed and she seems to have doubted whether she was truly loved if her husband could leave her to undertake what she knew was a dangerous mission. Flinders replied that he sympathized with her and only wished he could transport himself to her to comfort her, and went on to say:

My dearest friend, thou adducest my leaving thee to

follow the call of my profession, as a poor proof of my affection for thee. Dost thou not know, my beloved, that we could have barely existed in England? That both thou and me must have been debarred of even necessaries; unless we had given up our independence to have procured them from perhaps unwilling friends. It was only upon the certainty of obtaining an employment, the produce of which would be adequate to thy support as well as my own, that I dared to follow the wishes of my heart and press thee to be mine. Heaven knows with what sincerity and warmth of affection I have loved thee, how anxiously I look forward to the time when I return to thee, and how earnestly I labour that the delight of our meeting may be no more clouded with fear of long parting. Do not then, my beloved, adduce the following of the dictates of necessity as my crime. Rather, my dearest Ann let us submit to what has been deemed for us and look forward with our best hopes to the good which is in store for us.

Towards the end of July the preparations were nearing completion. During the stay in Port Jackson thorough cleaning and re-painting was done, the provisions that had been sent out from England were taken aboard, wood and water loaded, the water casks having been checked by the cooper. Nevertheless, some time ashore was allowed, which may have accounted for Francis Smith and Joseph Tozo, who had only recently been entered, being punished with lashing for drunkenness and fighting. On another occasion, a seaman from the whaler *Greenwich*, who appears to have been lent to work on the *Investigator* whilst in port, was punished, with permission from his own Master, with eighteen lashes for mutinous expressions and striking the Mate. Afterwards the ship's company were mustered, seen to be clean and some were sent ashore to attend Divine Service, it being Sunday. Compared with punishment by lashing meted out in many ships of the time, Flinders resorted to it on only a very few occasions.

Three convict ships arrived during the time the *Investigator* was in port. About one of the ships no comment was made, but of another Flinders remarked on the sickly appearance of the men and that sixty had died on the way out. The third convict ship to arrive was the *Hercules* from Cork and an entry is made that the Commander and First Lieutenant of the *Investigator* sat as members of a Court of Vice Admiralty to try Mr. Lukyn Betts, Master of the *Hercules*, for putting to death several convicts said to be concerned in a mutinous attempt to take the ship from the commander and officers.

John Aken, the Mate of the *Hercules*, transferred to the *Investigator* — probably only too happy to do so — and he was appointed Master to replace Thistle. Five seamen from other ships also joined. However, six had been lost in the accident at Cape Catastrophe and in any case they had left England with four fewer seamen than was ideal. Therefore, the Governor gave permission for nine convicts to be taken on, who were told they would receive conditional or absolute pardons on their return according to Flinders' recommendation. Two natives of Sydney also volunteered, namely Bongaree, who had been in the *Norfolk* for the expedition to Moreton Bay, and a younger man named Nambaree.

In the early part of July a report[2] was completed setting out what had been achieved during the stay at Port Jackson.

The ship's company had been refreshed and provision made for what would be a twelve months' expedition along

---

[2] See Note 2 for the complete report.

the coast, but it was said that it had been necessary to trust to the individual exertions of the crew rather than to public purchases, the price of fresh food being exorbitant. A thorough examination had been made of all the stores with time for the different officers to pass their accounts.

The charts had been made up and a midshipman had been given the task of making copies. This was to ensure that if the ship taking the charts back to England failed to get home, second copies would be kept safely by the Governor at Port Jackson for the time being.

Careful checking of the accuracy of the time keepers had been made and the greenhouse had been set up on the deck. The number of the crew had been brought up to strength to make up for the disastrous loss of the men at Cape Catastrophe and for the four men who had been discharged from active service.

Details appear about the purchase of 30,000 pounds of biscuit, 8,000 pounds of flour and 156 bushels of wheat. From two American ships that had arrived, 1,438¼ gallons of rum was bought at 6/6^d a gallon, and another purchase was made of 978 pounds of tobacco at 6^d a pound, which was considered good value.

An application was sent to the Admiralty for further ship's stores and food to be sent so that there would be a supply ready when the *Investigator* returned to port. Apart from more sails, an anchor, barrels of tar and other necessities for the maintenance of the ship, the food requested included salted meat, dried peas, sauerkraut, lime juice and mustard in bottles.

Two suits of sails which had been sent out from England were found to be damaged and the sail makers had spent considerable time in making repairs.

Discussions took place with the Governor about the next stage of the voyage to comply with the orders received from the Admiralty to find a better passage through the reefs and then make an examination of the northern coast. It was also ordered that the small survey ship, the *Lady Nelson* should accompany the *Investigator* and as he was to be under Flinders' orders, Lieutenant John Murray, her commander, was given a short code of signals to be observed.

On the 15th July Flinders wrote that through the Governor's assistance they were able to leave Port Jackson in a better state than when they left England with not a man on the sick list.

The two months in harbour away from battering winds and seas had not been idle, but they would have been a break from the lonely and unremitting responsibilities of a captain taking a ship across the world and into unknown waters. Flinders had been able to be in constant touch with Governor King who gave him great encouragement and who wished him well as the *Investigator* slipped out to the open sea on the 21st July 1802.

7

The First Circumnavigation

Heading northwards from Sydney Harbour not much time was taken in passing the part of the coast on which Cook and Flinders had been before, but some corrections to the charts were made. An opportunity was taken to go ashore so that the botanists might look for plants and contact be made with local people. Meeting with some of them who were suspicious, Bongaree, who always went with Flinders in the boat, went towards them alone, having laid down his hunting spear and taken off his clothes so that they realised there was nothing to fear. They were given presents and twenty of them came down to the shore where they enjoyed a feast of blubber.

On 5th August a wide bay was found behind an island which Cook had missed by passing it in the night. It was named after Sir Roger Curtis, the Admiral at Cape Town, who had been so helpful during the stay there, and because the entrance was hazardous Flinders wrote instructions for future mariners to approach with caution with a boat ahead and a plan upon the binnacle.

As Cook never went back to the point which he had left when darkness fell, the ship could drift and so there were gaps in his chart. Flinders always returned to the exact point he had left the previous evening, which apart from his meticulous draughtsmanship is the reason why his charts are so accurate. Nevertheless, he had to make a correction to his own chart made at Cape Moreton when in the *Norfolk* where he found he had missed a reef out to sea, where any vessel would have been considered safe. Again he missed the mouths of the Clarence and Brisbane rivers. To those accustomed to the wide mouths of English rivers this may seem extraordinary, but the curve of the land, the large sandbanks and dense mangrove swamps choking the estuary through which the river meandered made it difficult to see from a ship, even if near to the shore. It may also be remembered that James Cook had not thought to explore the great harbour that was to become Sydney and had altogether missed its importance, although it was open to the sea.

On making a measurement on the run across Hervey Bay Flinders found it to be 43 miles, whereas Cook had found it 59 miles wide. Measuring very carefully he found that Cook's measurements were often inaccurate – by the time they reached Cape York the measure was out by 35 miles and Flinders was to write that the position of almost every island was different to Cook's chart, which "caused much perplexity and uneasiness". Flinders did have the benefit of chronometers and whilst he may have regretted that his hero Cook, had been less than perfect, it fell to him to correct the charts, which made a significant difference to future navigation and safety.

Flinders continued to test his theory on the movements of the barometer being affected by the winds, the mercury going down as the onshore winds died away indicating that the ship could safely stay at anchor overnight and only a mile from shore instead of having to sail further out and then return to the same spot at dawn, which would save much time and effort and mean greater accuracy.

By mid-September they were heading for Keppell Bay and the Tropic of Capricorn. This was a very difficult coastline to explore with its shoals and mangrove swamps through which they had to fight their way before reaching dry land. Flinders wished to climb a hill, as he often did in order to get a better view of the surrounding area, but he failed because of the dense undergrowth and said it would have been easier to climb the trees and scramble across the vines on top. The botanists were disappointed as they did not discover anything new and on one occasion two of them got separated from the others. They spent the night tormented by mosquitoes, but were found in the morning by local people who gave then a meal of duck and showed them the way back to the ship.

At Broad Sound Brown recorded being badly stung by plants and he also identified a moderate sized tree which he described as carrying both flowers and capsules (the crow's ash) and naming it Flindersia australis.

Whilst at Broad Sound on the 17th September it was thought advisable to check the absolute accuracy of the time-keepers by taking them on shore before the serious exploratory work began. To do this, Samuel Flinders was left in charge and with some others was to camp on the shore for about a week, whilst Lieutenant Murray was to supervise the repairs to the keel of the *Lady Nelson* which had been damaged. Flinders took the *Investigator* to Thirsty Sound where he and the botanists explored the area, but on return it was found that Samuel had excelled himself.

For some time Flinders had been doubting the wisdom of taking his younger brother with him on the voyage as his lazy manner could cause friction. When they had arrived on the southern coast the previous December Samuel complained he had to work too hard. As Crosley, the astronomer, whose assistant he was, had to be left behind in South Africa, he did have to do extra work in order to help his brother who had to take on the responsibility of Crosley's duties. For the commander's young brother to behave thus could not be allowed, and he had to be disciplined.

On this occasion, on return to Broad Sound they found that Samuel had let the chronometers stop having been carried away with calculations measuring the distance between the moon and the sun. He was in many ways as good or even better a mathematician than his elder brother, genuinely interested in lunar calculations. The complicated business of re-setting the clocks took at least five days because it was a matter of fine-tuning to get them synchronised. Samuel was left to work on his observations and to re-set and check the clocks for another four days, whilst Flinders rejoined the botanists. On return Flinders found to what he called his surprise and regret, that again the clocks had not been wound. This was serious as they could not afford the time to get the clocks accurate and so had to continue "with the best rates we could scrape together". It is interesting to note that although Samuel's name is given in the journal recording the daily events, Flinders in recounting the incident loyally omits it in "The Voyage to Terra Australis" which was intended for general publication. Nevertheless, the atmosphere at dinner must have been a little tense.

The most dangerous part of the voyage was about to begin. It was time to leave the coast and head for the Northumberland Islands known to Cook. In 1770 Cook had negotiated a passage through the coral reefs and rocks, during the course of which he had severely damaged his ship, the *Endeavour*. Being a moonlit night the ship kept sailing as was Cook's custom, with the leadsman continually measuring the depth of water. He called out seventeen fathoms, but as he swung the lead again there was a splintering noise as the ship struck a hidden reef. Cook rushed on deck in his nightshirt to direct operations. The tide was falling and when it rose again the ship moved, but in spite of the guns being thrown overboard to lighten the weight, could not be brought off the reef until the second high tide. Water was pouring in and everyone had to take a turn manning the pumps, including the officers and Joseph Banks. There was a gaping hole and it was due to a young man, Jonathan Monkhouse, who having seen it done before when crossing the Atlantic, suggested that the ship should be fothered, that is to say bandaged with sailcloth on to which large tufts of oakum were stitched, the pressure of the incoming water forcing the sail into the hole. They were then able to sail on until a suitable place was found on the mainland to run ashore to make extensive repairs. Cook was generous in his praise of the crew and Banks wrote "The seamen worked with surprising chearfulness and alacrity. No grumbling or growling was to be heard throughout the ship, not even an oath (though the ship in general was as well furnished with them as most in his Majesty's service)".

Troubles were not over as shortly after the *Endeavour* was repaired and re-floated the wind dropped and she was becalmed. The sea was too deep to find an anchorage and in spite of lowering boats, keeping the ropes attached and with teams of men rowing to try to draw the ship back, the strong tide was taking her nearer and nearer to the reefs until she was right in the breakers. By a miracle, what Banks described as "a friendly little breeze" got up and they were saved, but both he and Cook recorded afterwards that they thought they were facing death.

Cook went on northwards through dangerous waters to prove that what we now call Far North Queensland and New Guinea were separated by the sea — the Torres Strait called after the Spaniard Luis Vaes de Torres, who in 1606 is thought to have sailed through the Strait and to have sighted the hills of Cape York, but for some unknown reason this had been kept a secret until his papers were discovered in Manila.

Flinders' orders were to sail up the eastern coast and to try to find a better passage for future use of shipping before making a survey of the northern coast, and he knew full well the dangers that existed in the area he named the Great Barrier Reef, through which he had to navigate.

From 4th October they were in constant danger with shadows from white clouds, patches of water tinged green, ripplings and shoals making it difficult to distinguish whether there were reefs just below the surface and the whale boat had to be sent ahead.

11th October

All the reefs passed this afternoon were nearly dry and showed themselves distinctly. The situation where we anchored in the evening is some miles to the eastward of the reefs upon which the sea was seen to break high on the 7th. PM; but we had the satisfaction to see it breaking here also, upon shoals a little over the great front bank. This and the appearance of two openings though they were small led me to the hope for the speedy termination of the time, which I now consider us to be losing from more important employments.

A.M. On approaching the opening which promised fairest to let us out to sea, it appeared that there were small patches of reef lying in it, and the soundings all about it were very irregular and the bottom bad. Out to sea the prospect was by no means so good as when it was less distinct; for although there were no dry banks visible, yet breakers appeared to a considerable distance out to sea beyond what I had supposed to be the front bank. The rapidity of the tide and consequent badness of the bottom makes the attempting these small channels to be very dangerous. We ran much risk in this attempt, and the loss of an anchor to each vessel is sufficiently serious to deter me from making any more such attempts.

One morning at daylight it was found that the ship had drifted about two miles towards the reefs. The commander's journal records, "This had not been perceived by the watch, a neglect that might have proved fatal to us, and which I am determined not to pardon a second time. The officer of the middle watch is the person to whom I attribute the blame".

In despair and feeling trapped, Flinders turned back to the Percy Islands and sailed along the inner side of the reef, still thinking there must be a gap. The Cumberland Islands, which Cook had named, were reached and some time spent there, Flinders and Westall staying a night on an island and because of the strong currents having difficulty in returning to the ship. Everyone on board was fascinated by the coral reefs and "the beauty of the scene although so pregnant with destruction to seamen".

Scientists had been interested for some time about the formation of coral reefs in the warmer waters of the world and in describing the reefs he saw Flinders wrote:-

> It seems to be that when the animalcules which form the corals at the bottom of the ocean cease to live, their structures adhere to each other, by virtue either of the glutinous remains within, or of some property in salt water.

He went on to describe how:

> the next generation of these animalcules build on the rising bank and die in their turn, to increase, but

principally to elevate, this monument of their wonderful labours.

He continued that he thought when they finally broke the surface, and so only got washed by tides, they lost their adhesive property and remained in a loose state forming what he called a key on the top of the reef. Before long sea birds would arrive and land birds would visit, depositing the seeds of shrubs and trees.

The form of an island is gradually assumed: and last of all comes man to take possession.

In 1842 Charles Darwin when writing his treatise on the Structure and Distribution of Coral Reefs was to make use of Flinders' charts and his descriptions.

The details written in the journal during the time spent in the area make it only too clear the dangers they faced night and day. Nevertheless, orders were carried out for the daily tasks of seeing to the general running of the ship, the food, the hygiene and the water supply, the washing of hammocks. The usual twice weekly entry "Mustered the ship's company and saw them clean" is entered. At one point when in the Northumberland Islands a search had to be made for fresh water, knowing that it was likely to become increasingly difficult to find for the time being and it was essential to have it in the heat. A gully was found with good water, but in order to get it, twenty five men spent a day cutting through a quarter of a mile of mangroves so that the huge casks could be rolled down to the shore, lifted into a boat and "thus get the ship completed with this necessary article". The language used by the seamen in describing the day's work might have been a little less elegant.

All observations had to be recorded and as often as possible Flinders joined the scientists and the two artists to study not only the shore line and rock formations, but the plants, trees, animals and birds, and make peaceful contact with the native Australians. The officers remaining aboard had to keep a continuous watch as the safety of the ship was paramount. In addition to the orders issued as the *Investigator* left England, Flinders issued further orders on the 10th October to emphasise what was required of the officers.

General Orders

1st. When the ship is in the neighbourhood of land, reefs, or any other danger, the boatswain, gunner and carpenter are to have the charge of the look out at night upon the forecastle; and under the officer of the watch are to be responsible for any <u>unseen</u> danger that the ship may get into during their look out. Also, in particular situations, which will be pointed out by the Commander, the said officers are to look out from the top-gallant yard in the day time, holding themselves answerable as before.

2nd. When any land or danger is in sight, the officer of the watch is to visit the mast head at the end of his watch in the daytime, and report to the Commander what is in sight from thence; and when a warrant officer is not there, the mate of the watch is to do the same in the middle of the watch and report to the officer.

Still off the Cumberland Islands Flinders came to a decision about the *Lady Nelson*. Even before leaving England he had had doubts as to whether a small accompanying ship was likely to be of use, and that possibly the use of a whaleboat for inshore work would be more practical. At Port Jackson he may have reflected on the fact that the *Le Géographe* and *Le Naturaliste* had lost each other on two occasions, but his orders had been to take the *Lady Nelson* with him. He was proved right and the *Lady Nelson* would have been useless in the Gulf of Carpentaria. Now her keel had been damaged, repaired and damaged again and she had lost two anchors, added to which her inability to keep up made her a liability and it was decided that she should return to Port Jackson, although Flinders much regretted having to disappoint her commander, Lieutenant Murray, who had done his best to make himself and his vessel useful. Before parting some members of the crews were exchanged and young Nambaree, having asked to go home, went on board the *Lady Nelson*. A quantity of stores was transferred to the *Investigator*, together with a five oared boat, and Murray was entrusted to carry back official reports for the Governor and a letter to Ann was slipped in as well.

Investigator off the Cumberland Isles

October 18, 1802.

My dearest love, up to this day we are all well and the accomplishment of the objects of the voyage is advancing prosperously.

Amidst my various and constant occupations, thou art not one day forgotten. Be happy my beloved, rest assured of my faith and trust that I will return safely to soothe thy distresses, and repay thee for all thy anxieties concerning me.

Beg thy good father and mother to accept my affectionate and respectful regards, as well as my friend Belle, and believe me to be thy own.

Matthew Flinders.

I have no time to write to my father — do thou for me.

Having shown the colours when parting the *Lady Nelson* turned southwards. She had a troublesome run back, losing another anchor. The carpenter shaped a very large piece of wood to which he attached two of the guns and this served as a make-shift anchor, and they arrived safely at Port Jackson.

The *Investigator* tacked to the northward in fine weather, keeping well away from the reefs, but looking for a safe way through. Smith wrote in his account that "We proceeded on the Voyage with our Usual Alacrity" which was in contrast to his comment that the *Lady Nelson* was "a Dull sailing Vessel".

Flinders had hoped to return to the area to survey more carefully this part of the north-east coast, but he was never able to do so.

Meeting with the same baffling confusion of rocks and shoals, Flinders was clearly glad that he had made the decision to send the *Lady Nelson* home writing that "had the brig been ahead of the ship this evening without seeing the shoal water before us, as is probable she would not, it would have gone hard with her, for she certainly could not have weathered the point of the reef, and indeed to have lain at anchor where we did, into such a breeze and swell and a reef under the lee, would have but ill suited with want of a second anchor".

The following night the wind got up and there was too much swell to think of anchoring and so, although the risk was great, they kept under sail all night. On the 21st Flinders was in a dilemma. Caution told him to veer westwards to find a safer place to anchor at night, but from the way the waves were breaking on the reefs he suspected that there was at last an opening, and by eight o'clock in the evening there was no doubt they were through and into the open sea but the weather was too rough to allow a detailed look at the reefs facing the Pacific. Flinders was to write "that any man whose nerves were not strong enough to thread his way directing the steerage from the masthead would be recommended not to approach this part of New South Wales."

From reading the journal recorded daily it is possible to understand the tension and the dangers they faced, which their commander was determined should be overcome. It was part of that fever of discovery.

* * *

Heading northwards in the open sea gave a few days respite before turning westwards to face the next challenge.

In September 1792 William Bligh, commanding *H.M.S. Providence* with young Midshipman Flinders aboard, had negotiated a passage into the Torres Strait from the Pacific. Bligh was a superb navigator and had to twist and turn through islands and rocks for nineteen days before he and his accompanying ship were safely through to the Timor Sea. Whilst a great feat of seamanship, this was not a passage that could in the future be used by general shipping and neither was Cook's passage up the mainland coast round Cape York. An attempt to find a better way through was tried by William Bampton and Matthew Alt in 1793 and had taken seventy two days.

Before the *Investigator* entered the Torres Strait the Murray Islands were visited, where three long canoes appeared, manned by some fifty natives. Flinders having witnessed the experience that Bligh had had and knowing that Bampton and Alt had had a difficult encounter, the *Investigator*'s guns were kept turned on the canoes, but all was well and gifts were exchanged. Next day seven canoes came alongside and again, so as to ensure that future ships would receive a peaceful reception, gifts were made. Not certain who was the chief man, Flinders offered to the oldest man a hand saw, a hammer and nails "all of which we attempted to show him how to use, but I believe without success: for the poor old man became frightened on finding himself so particularly noticed".

Continuing towards the centre of the Torres Strait they were well away from the tracks of either Bligh to the north or Cook to the south.

31st October

When compared to the track of any preceding navigator through this strait, our run this afternoon has been almost in clear water. I trusted to the judgement of my officers and myself for distinguishing the shoals from the mast head, and ran whilst the wind served us.

An island on which they landed is then described

The little isle is occasionally visited by men, who obtain here the fruit of the pandanus, and the gigantic cockles from the reef. Numbers of these shells were placed under the trees, evidently for the purpose of catching fresh water; there being strips of bark round the trees to lead the water into them and the shade of the tree prevents its exhalation in some measure: the shells were half full of water at this time. I brought two shells on board whose weight, now quite clean and bleached is 101 pounds. The island is covered by shrubs and trees, and partly impenetrable. There are many pigeons upon it, but very shy. The rock is coarse coral sand caked and hardened. The island is not many feet above high-water mark and about 1 mile is its greatest circumference.

A.M. The clear run that we made this morning as far as the York Isles, being added to the former part of our passage through this strait, will tend to disarm this very formidable navigation of a great part of its terrors. The ground passed over this morning is everywhere fit to anchor upon, and much superior to what we have been accustomed to amongst the reefs of the east coast.

Approaching Cape York, the most northern point of what today is called Queensland, Flinders became increasingly concerned that Cook's measurements were not correct and it was imperative that the exact position of Cape York should be fixed.

It was hoped to anchor at the historic Possession Island of Captain Cook, where he had claimed possession of New South Wales in the name of the British Crown, but the rainy blustery weather made it necessary to anchor in the first safe place. The mainland could be seen to the south, but Flinders was confused not only by Cook's measurements but by three islands which did not appear on his charts. He sent Fowler off in the whale boat, when he reported that he had seen what he thought was Cook's Endeavour Strait to the south. So having finished his observations and his rough chart he continued westwards. On 3rd November he wrote in the journal that having climbed a hill he saw that these islands were indeed the Prince of Wales group "not withstanding the great difference of longitude from Captain Cook" — and then these words are neatly crossed out.

The islands were found to be well wooded with sheltered roadsteads but the tides ran very strongly among them. On other islands curious structures, resembling bell tents or white sentry boxes had been seen from the distance and now seeing them more closely they were found to be huge ants nests, some of them eight feet in height.

With no land now in sight to the west it was obvious they were through to the Timor Sea (Flinders called it the Indian Sea), and therefore, the mission to find a safer and direct passage from the Pacific to the Torres Strait had been successfully completed in six days. Flinders thought that with accurate charts it could be done in three days and he was proved right exactly a year later when again he came through the Strait.

This was a discovery of very great importance which would mean that ships from India and Africa instead of sailing the long way round the north coast of New Guinea, to reach the Pacific Ocean, could save weeks on the voyage. There was no means of getting the news to anyone and it was not until the following May that a report could be given to Governor King at Sydney, who was to call it "a matter of universal benefit". Flinders himself regarded it as an experiment and in March 1803 in a letter to Sir Joseph Banks he said he hoped that some use could be made of the discovery and that he had given the best directions he could for going through the strait in safety.

* * *

Turning south westwards the *Investigator* was to cross the track followed by Cook on his way from Endeavour Strait to Timor, and to enter the Gulf of Carpenteria. He would have liked to spend more time checking his charts of the Torres Strait, but knew that the monsoon would soon be breaking making this dangerous, if not impossible.

Everyone was in good spirits, but there was a serious cause for concern. Although it is recorded that sea conditions had been smooth, and they had been running under the topsails and jib only, the ship was leaking badly — six inches an hour, ten inches, and fourteen inches. It was obvious there were rotten timbers and apart from the continual pumping necessary, such timbers would be unlikely to survive a scrape with a submerged rock. It would be necessary to find a suitable place where repairs could be carried out in the more peaceful waters of the gulf.

The early Dutch explorers had known that this coast

existed and Flinders had with him an old chart believed to have been made by that renowned Dutch navigator, Abel Tasman in 1644. It seems it was more a representation of the shape of this extensive gulf with its indentations and spits of land rather than a detailed chart. It fell again to Flinders to produce a detailed and highly accurate chart. This cannot have been an easy task as in parts it was not possible to take the ship nearer than four miles and sometimes seven miles from the shore because of the extreme shallowness of the water.

On Sunday 7th November they attempted to explore a small river using the boat, but could not get up further than 1¼ miles, although they could see up a greater distance. On the northern shore sixteen natives were seen, carrying spears and sticks and having with them a small canoe, but no contact was made and so two hatchets were left on the bank as gifts. As the *Investigator* continued along the coast many smokes from fires were seen, indicating that the land was populated.

Reddish cliffs came in view and then the coastline became lower with trees and shrubs but rising behind them was smoke, so it seemed likely that further inland the country was fertile and inhabited, but because of the sandy shoals it was necessary to keep well away from the water's edge and therefore it was difficult to judge.

> The land which we have sailed along this day and on that preceding, has, if possible, been still lower than the more northern parts of the coast. The present direction which the shore takes, as well as the great shallowness of the water shew that we are near the head of the gulph, and consequently that the old charts have thus far given its form with tolerable accuracy. — Since losing sight of the Prince of Wales' Isles, I do not think that we have seen any land so high as a ships masthead, which

is an extent of coast more than equal to 400 miles — an instance that will scarcely be equalled by any coast in any part of the world; and as the same thing still continues, it may perhaps go on much further.

They had reached the southerly part of the coastline which began to curve north west, with large dry shoals along the shore, and it became clear that there was no arm of the sea into the interior that could even partly divide the continent, and the theory that there were two large islands could be absolutely dismissed. Nevertheless because they had to keep well away from the coast and its sandbanks it was difficult to identify the small rivers, which were marked on the old Dutch charts.

Two days later a landing was made to find a place where water casks could be rolled down and re-filled, but without success. However, signs of fires were found, with fish bones and oyster shells scattered about together with a hole in the ground divided into two compartments, each big enough for a man to lie in, and a seven foot length of teakwood which the carpenter thought might have come from the quarter deck of a ship of some size.

Still looking for water unsuccessfully on the 20th November the "botanical gentlemen" went ashore to examine plants and Flinders took the boat on to a nearby island where there was a sandy beach on which some men were seen dragging rafts to the water and then making off towards a group of rocks. Always hoping to make peaceful contact with local people, Flinders went towards them and later described their appearance by saying their legs did not bear the European proportion to the size of their heads and bodies. Although their features were similar to the inhabitants of Port Jackson, instead of being without one upper tooth, these men had two front teeth missing.

After being five minutes with them, the two elder proposed to go to the boat. They walked along hand in hand; but presently they turned back, and after making a short speech which concluded with the word jahre, pronounced with emphasis, they returned to the rafts, and dragged them towards their three companions upon the rocks. Flinders thought that these three were women, and that the going of the men to the boat was only a feint. He questioned whether the women were so much afraid, as on their account the men seemed to be, for on walking back as far out as possible, he saw the three women, very quietly knocking oysters off the rocks, although the distance between them was then less than before.

Two days later the *Investigator* reached a point where it was thought suitable to stay for a few days to make repairs. The carpenters got to work but their report was far from good. Some patching up was done so that they could sail on hoping to find a better place to stop for a longer time, but this they failed to do and returned to the passage between Sweer's Island and Bentinck's Island. Surprisingly plenty of clear water was found and wasting no time it was loaded and Flinders and the scientists went ashore, whilst the carpenters began their thorough examination of the whole ship. Their findings of the rotten state of much of the timber was very serious to a point where they said that in a strong gale and a heavy sea the ship would be likely to founder and that if driven on shore might go to pieces. They believed that in twelve months there would scarcely be a sound timber left, but that given fine weather she might run for six months without a great risk.

Their report stated:-

1st. The ship having before made ten inches of water an hour in a common fresh breeze, we judge from that and what we have now seen, that a little labouring would employ two pumps; and that in a strong gale with much sea running the ship would hardly escape foundering; so that we think she is totally unfit to encounter much bad weather.

2nd. We have no doubt but that if the ship should get on shore under any unfavourable circumstances, she would immediately go to pieces; but with a soft bottom and smooth water she might touch for a short time without any worse consequences than to another ship, if she did not heel much; but altogether, we judge it to be much more dangerous for her to get aground in her present state than if she was sound.

3rd. It is our opinion that the ship could not bear heaving down on any account; and that laying her on shore might so far strain her as to start the copper and butt ends, which would make her unable to swim without vast repair.

4th. Mr Aken has known several ships of the same kind and built at the same place as the Investigator, and has always found that when they began to rot they went on very fast. From the state to which the ship now seems to be advanced, it is our joint opinion, that in from eight to twelve months there will scarcely be a sound timber in her; but that if she remains in fine weather and happens no accident, she may run six months longer without much risk. — We are, Sir,

John Aken — master

Russel Mart — carpenter.

To   Mattw. Flinders Esq.

Commander of H.M. sloop Investigator.

Flinders immediately realized that he was facing a serious crisis. His plan to make a detailed survey of the rest of the northern and western coast would be impossible without enormous risk to the lives of all on board and the possible loss of the work he had done if they foundered. They would have to return to Port Jackson either to get another and sounder ship which would take buffeting about in stormy waters or wait in Port Jackson while the ship was virtually rebuilt, which would take many months and probably not be at all satisfactory. For the moment they were in a lonely trap having seen only the sails of two distant ships since they left Port Jackson, one of which was believed to be *Le Géographe*.

On 26th November he wrote despairingly:

> The condition of the ship being according to the above statement, it surprised me that some discovery of it should not have been made when the ship was in dock at Sheerness, or when she was caulked at the cape of Good Hope, or at Port Jackson when the barricade was removed: this is accounted for to me as follows. — that two years back when the ship underwent repair in dock, she could not be a quarter part so bad as she now is, and that the shipwrights did not examine her with a view to such a voyage as the present, but to common short voyages near home. When she was caulked at the Cape, she was not then near so bad as at present; and as nothing was done to her but caulking, and no suspicion entertained of her being rotten, it is no wonder that it was not found out, since it is probable that it might not have been now discovered, if the rottenness of the plank had not begun to affect the outer parts. At Port Jackson the barricade was removed and many timbers consequently laid open, but these were what had been let in to support the barricade which was built only when the ship was taken into His Majestys service, and were no part of the ship in her original construction.

> From the above dreadful state of the ship, I find the complete examination of this country, which is one of the nearest objects to my heart, to be greatly impeded,

if not destroyed. I have hitherto considered that my business is to make so accurate an examination of New Holland, that there shall be no necessity for any further navigator to come after me; and with this view we have till now kept close to the shore and run many other risks that we might not miss to see every thing and with the blessing of God, I would not have left any thing of import to be discovered hereafter upon any of the shores of this great country; but with a ship which cannot encounter bad weather, which cannot be repaired if her bottom meets with the least accident, and which, if we could command constant fine weather and be certain to avoid accidents, will not run more than six months, with such a ship I do not know how to prosecute so great an undertaking. For the present, however, I determined to go on in the examination of this gulph, if the N.W. monsoon does not prove too great an hindrance and afterwards to act as circumstances shall most require.

With the north west monsoon breaking with its severe storms and cyclones it was out of the question to return the way they had come through the reef given the weak state of the ship. It was only slightly less dangerous to venture westwards and then continue round the southern coast again.

With absolute determination to chart and examine the Gulf of Carpentaria, Flinders decided they would finish this task while the monsoon continued and then as soon as fair winds returned they should either go straight back to Port Jackson by the western and southern coasts or make for the nearest port in the East Indies. He was bitterly disappointed, realizing his responsibility in whatever decisions had to be made, but supported by the whole ship's company. The cynic might say they had no choice but in fact they trusted him and most loyally gave him support. Smith did remark that they "Dispair'd of ever Arriving safe into any port, especially if we met with Boisterous Weather" and then calmly added that "those who chose was allowed to go on shore to Wash their Cloaths".

Whilst the re-caulking and all the repairs were taking place, shore parties were organised staying ashore at night. A well was sunk so that fresh water could be drawn to take back to the ship and firewood for the cooking stove was collected. Sleeping in tents was probably a much enjoyed break after the stuffy conditions of the lower deck and the small cabins of the officers. The thermometer showed temperatures of between 81° and 90° Fahrenheit, but as there was a breeze, it was seldom oppressive and the insects were said not to be very troublesome. The opportunity was taken to check on shore the accuracy of the chronometers and the range of mercury in the barometer. The scientists were busy on the two islands between which they were anchored and a supply of fresh fish could be had for everyone to eat, although with ninety men on board a great deal would have had to be caught to relieve the monotony of the ship's diet. They did see a few local people who kept well away, but on Sweer's Island they found seven human skulls and a number of bones. On Bentick's Island they came across a broken earthenware jar and noticed that trees had been cut down recently, so it was concluded that there had been some unwelcome visitors.

By the 1st December, with some difficulty, the ship was able to leave what was to be called Investigator Road and they continued the survey. Near the point which Tasman had called Cape van Diemen (but which turned out to be an island) a large quantity of turtle was caught, which again supplemented the dreary and by now rather stale diet of biscuits and salted pork and may have helped to compensate for the monsoon conditions with temperatures averaging 85° Fahrenheit, heavy squalls of wind and rain with thunder, and the plagues of mosquitoes and worse still black flies which got into the mouth and nose and settled on eyelids. The tediousness of the featureless coastline was occasionally relieved by low groups of islands on some of which strange charcoal-burning fireplaces were found and also more earthenware jars, three broken rudders, which seemed to be of Asian design and a curious length of black rope made of what appeared to be hair and resembling ropes used in the East Indies. A small shack was also found made of palm leaves sewn together with cotton thread and which looked like the top of an umbrella or a Chinese hat.

On another day, whilst again looking for fresh water some roughly made rudders were found and a small anchor made in the Malay or Chinese fashion and what appeared to be a shelter that had been used on a boat. It was made partly of teak and partly of violet wood which had a pleasant smell. Nearby they found a pair of cotton trousers of a style worn by Chinese.

Christmas Day was spent by Flinders and the scientists exploring in a boat and they sailed again on 27th December to continue charting. On New Year's Day, Flinders described an island believed to be one Tasman called Cape Maria and he noted the two regular sets of tide in twenty four hours, but the lead told nothing of which was the ebb or flood as the rise seemed trifling. On 4th January there was an accident in the whaleboat and one of the seamen, William Murray was drowned; unfortunately it was to be the first of a number of deaths that were to occur and was a sad start to the year 1803 — a year that was to prove so disastrous.

That day some distant hills were seen and two days later

Flinders felt certain that this was Groote Eyland, named by Abel Tasman. Here they stayed two weeks continuing the daily surveying and charting and Flinders attempted to climb the cliffs to get a better view of the neighbouring land, but it proved impossible because of large chasms and openings in which nutmeg trees shot up to about forty feet before branching out to produce their nuts which then fell down to the ground. There was also a quantity of jambo trees, the acid fruit of which was very refreshing in the heat and which they called apples.

As they surveyed Blue Mud Bay behind the island there was no sign of living people but Brown came across several skeletons, standing upright in hollow trees with the bones painted in red and white. The most sensational event was the finding, on what was named Cavern or Chasm Islet, caves which were decorated with coloured drawings of a group of men hunting kangaroo and drawings of turtle and porpoises. William Westall was sent to make copies of them and so was the first European artist to make a record of Aboriginal art.

However, it was on the main island that they ran into trouble. A party having landed to collect wood, a marine, Benjamin Morgan, was taken ill and although brought back to the ship he died that evening apparently from sunstroke. At one o'clock in the afternoon some natives were seen in a canoe: they landed and went up a hill following one of the scientists and his servant, who retreated and joined the party collecting wood. The natives came down and several seamen went towards them in a friendly manner. From a rather confused account it seems they first retreated and then came back when a master's mate, named Whitewood went towards them: thinking one of them was offering his spear to him he stretched out his hand to receive it, whereupon he was stabbed in the chest. He fired his musket, but did not harm anyone and turning back he was stabbed again three times, and the natives started throwing spears. More muskets were fired and the attackers ran away and it did not seem that any of them were wounded — indeed they stopped to pick up a sailor's hat. Westwood was taken back to the ship and he did recover, but unfortunately there was another skirmish in which one of the natives was killed. Flinders much regretted what had happened but thought that the men from the *Investigator* must have been seen from the mainland and that the natives had come over with the obvious intention of driving them away because they had experienced some aggressive visitors.

Sailing on towards Cape Arnhem, the country is described as flat and sandy with a few low hills of reddish colour. A fresh water lagoon was found where there was a quantity of duck and fowl and marks of humans, dogs and kangaroo were seen.

A landing was made in Arnhem South Bay early in the morning of 4th February when about twelve natives ran down to the shore to greet them and Bongaree was made especially welcome. The scientists walked towards some sand hills and were followed and the opportunity was taken of snatching a hatchet from one of the scientists' servants, running off with it, but returning when little notice was taken of this. They continued to be friendly, putting their arms round their visitors, but again snatched a musket and ran away. A shot was fired but had no effect except to make them run faster. When some of them came down to the tents which had been put up on the shore, what is described as an interview took place to persuade them to bring back the musket when they would be given a hatchet. It was brought back although the ramrod had gone, the stock broken and it was wet and full of sand.

They stayed around the tents and efforts were made to learn words of their language, "the restored harmony appearing to be perfect" but another hatchet was stolen, and they appeared to be determined to steal anything. Perhaps this was an illustration of the cultural clash that was to develop between native people who had no sense of personal possession and the European settlers of the future to whom personal possession was of importance. In any event they had learned the usefulness of a hatchet.

Fowler was ordered to keep a watch and to seize two natives and after some time to release one of them, making it clear that the other would not be released until the hatchet and other things were returned. Towards the evening Flinders went ashore to the tent and took the young captive, whose name was Woga, into the boat and then rowed towards a place where a group of natives had collected. Two came forward, bringing a girl with them who apparently they were offering to Bongaree perhaps in the hope that they would then be allowed to keep the hatchet, but it was made clear that the hatchet must be given back, and Woga joined in to enforce the request. They were told that the thief, Yehangare, had been beaten and had run away.

It seemed no hatchets were to be returned that night, so Woga was taken on board ship with a promise that he would be taken to the tent in the morning. After protesting, he ate a meal, laughed a lot, and having a free run of the ship took a great interest in the pigs, sheep and cats on board, animals which he would never have seen before. In the morning Woga was taken back to the tent but tried to run away, so he had to be bound when after some shouting to Bongaree he quietened down.

The botanists party made an attempt to work, but they

were obstructed by another group of natives and so returned to the ship. As evening approached Flinders went ashore again and released Woga, giving him some presents and asking him to return the hatchet, but having walked two hundred yards, he started to run and was not seen again. They were about to leave but Flinders was anxious that there should be no ill feelings as he would not have wished the natives to fear others who might arrive upon the coast and therefore feel aggressive towards them. He particularly had in mind Nicolas Baudin.

Flinders wrote a description of this bleak coast with its low hills and others being visible further inland. There were areas of granite and sandstone impregnated with iron, at one point containing so much iron that the needle of the theodolite was turned round by a small piece of it. The soil seemed poor but there was a fair amount of vegetation which he described as luxuriant at that season, probably owing to the rain and heat, with coarse grass, but of a kind unlikely to be eaten by cattle. There was plenty of water, but again it was likely to be seasonal, and some eucalyptus and nutmeg trees were growing.

It was felt certain that the bay had had previous visitors from the fact that wood scattered about had been cut down with iron tools, of which the inhabitants seemed to know the usefulness to the extent that they would steal hatchets.

In describing the people it is remarked that they were of the same race as those at Port Jackson and King George's Sound. There were only a few words which were similar to Port Jackson language, and it is said that their manners were very different, particularly "their propensity to stealing, which as before mentioned, they practised upon us with much effrontery".

By the 17th February they reached Cape Wilberforce

(named later after William Wilberforce, who was helpful to Flinders when he returned to London). On the 19th they were to discover the answer to the mysterious fireplaces and detritus they had seen and confirm that strangers had been on the coast. In a bay on the north coast of Arnhem Land, they came across six small ships tied up and covered over. On hoisting their pennant and ensign, each ship hung up a white flag. On getting nearer "I sent Lieutenant Flinders in an armed boat to learn what they were". He was watched very carefully within musket shot and with all hands at quarters. On his return he reported that they were prows or praos from Macassar, and shortly afterwards the six captains came aboard. Fortunately the *Investigator's* cook was a Malay and was able to interpret.

They said they were part of a large group of sixty such ships working along this part of the coast, and five more ships were to arrive in the bay the following morning. Flinders remained suspicious that they might be a group of pirates as each man carried a knife, and a watch was kept on them all night. The following day further visits were exchanged and Pobasso, their leader, and the other five had no objection to drinking port and even taking a bottle back with them, although they said they were what Flinders called Mahometans. Pobasso explained that the ships belonged to the Rajah of Boni and that they had been visiting this coast for some years to search for trepang or sea cucumber. Divers collected them, they were dried and smoked, taken to Timor and finally sold to the Chinese who regarded them as a great delicacy. Whilst Flinders admired the seamanship of these men, making the voyage aided only by an old Dutch compass, he was concerned that they were probably aggressive and had made the native Australians fearful.

Before sailing on Flinders named the group of islands

the English Company Islands, probably in recognition of their financial help with provisions for the *Investigator's* voyage, but also thinking that with the good harbours, the large amount of wild nutmeg and the trepang, there might be an opportunity for the company to extend its trading to this area.

Another two weeks were spent surveying the coast, the monsoon with its storms was over and the time had arrived to make a decision about discontinuing the exploration in order to get back to Port Jackson before the six months would be up from the date of the inspection of the ship in November. This was the limit that the ship would be likely to be seaworthy, given good weather, and in the knowledge that by the time the Bass Strait was reached the weather was likely to be rough.

The responsibility for surveying rested on the commander and he wrote that he was disabled, by scorbutic sores on his feet, from going to the masthead or making expeditions in a boat and any serious exploration would not be possible.

Therefore, on 6th March, Flinders took that decision, although with the greatest reluctance, and wrote that the survey of the north western coast would have to be left for a future opportunity and that it would now only be possible to make an outline map of that part of the coast. He felt that "it shews but very little of that genuine spirit of discovery which contemns all danger and inconveniences with its gratification". It seemed depressing when considering that the wind would have been favourable for exploring the coast, especially as it was known that there were some good harbours and taking into consideration the use that could be made of them, given accurate charts, by trading ships from India, and of more use than the Gulf of Carpentaria.

However, everyone was exhausted and Bell, the surgeon,

was expressing concern having made an examination of each member of crew, many of whom were suffering from early stages of scurvy, with swollen gums and ulcers. There had been cases of dysentery and he said that it was only the high standard of hygiene that had prevented worse.

They had spent a hundred and five days charting the gulf with quite extraordinary accuracy and Flinders wrote "it will be remarked that the form of it, given in the old charts, is not very erroneous which proves that it may have been the result of real examination" which was a generous tribute to Abel Tasman's exploration one hundred and fifty years previously. Now with the change of wind the monsoon appeared to be over and the *Investigator* headed for Kupang, (Flinders spelt it Coepang) the nearest port in Timor, arriving there three weeks later without any untoward incident.

The reason for his deviation was that it was hoped that, after eight months at sea, it would be possible to buy fresh supplies of food, such as rice, peas, sugar and molasses and particularly fruit and vegetables in an attempt to mitigate the outbreak of scurvy on the long voyage back to Port Jackson. A short stay in port would have meant a lightening of duties for everyone.

During the voyage Flinders formed a plan for returning and wrote a report which, if a ship could be found, Lieutenant Fowler was to take to England, travelling as a passenger, and be instructed to ask the Admiralty to send out another ship to Port Jackson suitable for completing the survey of the remainder of the coast. Although made welcome by the Dutch Governor, there was no ship likely to be able to take Fowler and the best that could be done was to send a packet of reports and letters on a ship leaving for Batavia (Djakarta) in the hope that there might be some way of forwarding it. In his letter to Ann he assured her of his love, omitting to mention his own health, but mentioning that this time he was not going to be able to complete the survey.

There was not a great deal of food to be had in Kupang, except a large quantity of rice, and a supply of fruit and vegetables: the facilities for any repairs to the ship were completely inadequate.

Whilst in Kupang they found the graves of Riedle d'Ansborough, the gardener of *Le Géographe* and of David Nelson the gardener of the *Bounty*. The Officers of the *Investigator* were invited to dine with the Governor on the eve of their departure on the 7th April, when it was found that two men were missing. One was Mortlake who had joined the ship at Port Jackson, and the other was the Malay cook named Williams. This was reported to the Governor, but there was little to be done about it, and obviously they had their own reasons for not wanting to get back to Port Jackson. Another check was made in the morning but there was no sign of them. The anchor was weighed, the Governor saluted with eighteen guns and the *Investigator* sailed.

In his original Sailing Orders drawn up in June 1801 Flinders was required to examine the area off the coast of Timor and "as particularly as circumstances allow, the bank which extends itself from the Trial Rocks[1], towards Timor in the hope that by ascertaining the depth and nature of the surroundings thereon, great advantage may arise to the East India Company's ships, in case that passage should hereafter be frequented by them". A few days were spent therefore in this area, having found on examination that the

---

[1] So called because a ship named the *Trial* had foundered there in 1622.

state of decay of the *Investigator* had not increased much since the repairs at Sweer's Island, but although he felt that the Trial Rocks did exist, he found no trace of them along the line that such ships would need to take.

By 12th April they turned for the long voyage back to Sydney Cove, but not before the journal recorded that a number of men having eaten a quantity of fruit to counteract scurvy, were now suffering from diarrhoea. Flinders remarked that he seemed to be caught between Scylla and Charybdis. It is more likely that the water at Kupang was infected.

The *Investigator* rounded the western coast and sailing southwards they met cooler and fresher weather, bringing a welcome relief after the weeks of monsoon weather. They kept well away from the land to take advantage of the wind, and the sea was said to be too high for the ship to make good way any nearer.

Carrying as much sail as was possible in safety, given the condition of the ship, they were able to cover over a hundred miles a day, reaching Cape Leeuwin on 13th May. Along the southern coast measurements taken the year before were checked, and Flinders would have liked to finish his survey of Kangaroo Island, but because of the ill health of the crew he knew it was imperative to get to Port Jackson without delay. They landed only once to get fresh water and to check the accuracy of the clocks, and a rather unsuccessful attempt was made to shoot some birds so that fresh meat might be eaten. With the air temperature dropping the galley fire was kept going all night to help keep warm eighteen men on the sick list, but five of them died during the voyage, the last one just as they were nearing Sydney Heads. Each was buried at sea with what was called "the usual ceremony", after which the rather grisly business of selling the dead man's possessions took place.

They ran through a gale on 23rd May and finally reached the Bass Strait, and it is to be hoped that for all his anxiety Flinders would have had a moment to recall that great experience when he and Bass, with a crew of eight, had discovered the existence of that strait in 1798.

On reaching Port Jackson on 9th June 1803 they had sailed the 5,000 miles from Timor in exactly two months. It was a very different entry into the peaceful water of Sydney Cove to their arrival a year before, but they had made history being the first men to circumnavigate Australia, and that included the first native Australian to do so. Let it also not be forgotten that they were accompanied by that remarkable cat, Trim, who not only had his own supply of fresh food by keeping down the rats, but had contributed much to the morale of the ship's company.

8

The Ill-Starred Voyage

As Flinders limped with difficulty from the quay to Government House to make his official call there, his mind must have been churning with thoughts about how to proceed. His immediate care was to see to the welfare of his crew and Governor King at once ordered that the colony's surgeon arrange for eleven of them to be taken to the hospital, but for three of them it was too late and they died there: and Peter Good, who had so carefully tended the plant collection was too ill to be moved and died aboard the ship. For the others a good supply of fresh meat and vegetables was available and even a supply of wine, and they slowly recovered normal health, as did those remaining on board.

Flinders himself was quite seriously ill, but he continued to work. He gave the Governor the report made by the carpenters on the state of the ship and asked that an independent examination should be made. It was found that in parts it was possible to push a cane through the outer woodwork, and had they run into stormy weather along the southern coast the ship would have been unlikely to survive. The examiner's report stated categorically that the *Investigator* was not worth repairing. She was only built some six years or so previously and it will be remembered that on first inspecting her Flinders had expressed some doubts but was told that it was the only ship available. Hidden shoddy workmanship and poor timber which could not stand up to rough conditions were the root of the unseaworthy state which she was in.

What was to be done? Both the Governor and Flinders were anxious that the survey should be completed but of the few ships available at Port Jackson, none was suitable. It was suggested that they wait for the return from India of the Governor's ship the *Buffalo* although there was no certainty when that might be, and in any case she was hardly suitable for survey work. King considered that Flinders should take *HMS Porpoise* back to England and attempt to get a new ship properly equipped. Work began at once to put the *Porpoise* into a good state of repair. Although greatly in need of time to recover, Flinders stayed aboard the *Investigator* supervising the dreary task of unloading the ship, paying off the crew and finally taking down the pennant. The *Investigator*, reduced to a hulk, was to remain in the harbour.

On arrival at Port Jackson there had been a number of letters from home among them one telling him that his father had died which upset him greatly as there had been some friction between them and clearly he had hoped that when he returned home, having achieved so much, they would have been reconciled. Young Samuel was also upset but the news at least drew them together again. Flinders did find his younger brother irritating and unreliable and there had been some coolness on occasions. Happily there were letters from Ann. In a long reply he told her of the state of the ship and the crew, saying that he had been lame for about four months and "much debilitated in health, and I fear in constitution, but am now recovering". He went on to say that "Trim, like his master is becoming grey; he is at present fat and frisky, and takes meat from our forks with his former dexterity: he is commonly my bedfellow".

He then wrote passionately saying:

> Thou has shewn me how very ill I have requited thy
> tender love in several cases. I cannot excuse myself now;
> but plead for respite until my return when in thy dear
> arms I will beg for pardon and if thou cannot forgive
> me all, will have it sealed with ten thousand kisses. If I
> could laugh at the effusions of thy tenderness, it would
> be to the idolatrous language thou frequently usest to
> me. Thou makest an idol, and then worshippest it;
> and like some of the inhabitants of the East, thou also
> bestowest a little occasional castigation, just to let the
> ugly deity know the value of thy devotion. Thinkest
> thou not my dearest love that I shall be spoiled by thy
> endearing flatteries? I fear it, and yet can hardly part
> with one, so dear to me is thy affection in whatever
> way expressed.

It is a long letter expressing his love for her and it ends:

> My heart is with thee, and so soon as I can ensure for
> us a moderate portion of the comforts of life, thou
> wilt see whether love or ambition has the greater power
> over me.

> Before thou wast mine, I had engaged on this voyage:-
> without it we could not live. Thou knowest not the
> struggle in my bosom, before I consented to the
> necessity. There was no prospect of a permanent
> subsistence but in pursuing what I have undertaken,
> and I doubt not but that it will answer the end.

Flinders also wrote a letter to George Bass, leaving it with
the Governor to give him on his return to Port Jackson
but he was never to do so.

Preparations for the voyage home went on with a sense
of urgency. Unfortunately it was only possible to take
some of the *Investigator's* crew aboard the *Porpoise*. These
included Samuel Flinders, John Franklin, John Aken and

William Westall. The scientists Brown and Bauer felt they could profitably continue their work in New South Wales, but that if Flinders was not back in eighteen months they would take the first available ship to England although remaining under Admiralty orders. They did not waste time. Having again collected plants around Sydney Cove, Brown went to Tasmania and Bauer to Norfolk Island. By the time they left for England an additional 1200 plants had been identified and sketched and Bauer had worked up his sketches of many animals from koalas to bandicoots and platypus to parrots.

The rest of the *Investigator's* crew either elected to stay in Port Jackson or agreed to join one of the two ships which were to travel the first part of the voyage in convoy — namely the East India Company's ship the *Bridgewater* and the merchant ship the *Cato* both sailing by way of Batavia. Flinders was to travel as a passenger with Fowler in command although he was to take orders from Flinders in the area of the Torres Strait through which the other two ships were to follow to prove that the newly found passage would be much quicker than the northern route used up to that time. This may seem a strange arrangement but it must have been thought it would relieve Flinders of responsibilities and give him time to recover and to work on his charts and reports which he took on board with him. Westall also took his drawings and a selection of plant specimens chosen by Brown was loaded, the live ones being put into the greenhouse which was transferred from the *Investigator* and the dried ones and the seeds were packed in special baskets. On 10th August all was ready and the little convoy moved out of the harbour, the Governor accompanying them as far as the Heads.

For the first three days they made slow progress, but the wind picked up and on the third and fourth days they covered 260 miles and in seven days 745 miles, the intention being to sail out and head north but keeping away from the Great Barrier Reef before entering the Torres Strait. On 17th August a signal was seen from the *Cato* indicating land ahead, but the sounding showed no bottom at 80 fathoms. At 9.30 in the evening breakers were seen by the lookout of the *Porpoise.* Fowler immediately "hauled to the wind on the starboard tack, and tried to stay, but the ship not coming round took upon a reef, and coming broadside to it, beat up it and the foremast soon went over the side." In the confusion it was impossible to fire a gun or show a light but everyone shouted as loudly as they could to warn the other two ships. They did swing away but the *Cato* had to hove back to avoid collision with the *Bridgewater*, and so struck the reef, but allowing the *Bridgewater* to avoid it. Seeing the *Bridgewater* was safe they had no doubt that boats would be sent at first light.

Flinders told Fowler that he must get his charts and log books and try to take them to the safety of the *Bridgewater*. Although not in command of the ship, but as the most senior officer, Flinders was in a position to insist that Palmer, the commander of the *Bridgewater*, should take on board the crews of the two stricken ships. Although one side of the ship was on the reef, there was deep water on the other side and a boat was lowered, but had to push off as soon as possible to prevent being stove, and Flinders jumped overboard and swam to it. He then found that there was nothing with which to bale out and there were only two oars instead of four. Of the six men in the boat, only three knew how to handle it, the others being the armourer, a cook and a marine who were cowering under the thwarts. These were made to bale out with their hats and shoes as the waves broke over until they reached calm water just deep enough to float the boat. They could see the light of the *Bridgewater* but they realized that unless she tacked it would be impossible to get near enough to her. "As by her light we saw she was standing on, I determined to get back to the wreck leaving my charts et cetera in the boat, but the surf ran too high for this and therefore we kept rowing gently all night under the lee of the breakers". They were joined by the cutter which stayed close by through the night, burning some blue lights and believing they saw an answering light from the *Bridgewater*, although it may have been a general light showing, as it was not seen after 2.00 a.m.

As the morning dawned they rowed back to the *Porpoise* and Flinders waded across the reef because the ship had driven further on to it and the tide had fallen. By climbing on the fallen masts he was able to board the ship. It was then seen that what in the darkness they had thought were breakers was a white sandbank which was dry and large enough to land on and to take over provisions and equipment, and moreover they could see the *Bridgewater* which appeared to be coming towards them. Flinders left again in the small boat to go to a point where he could signal to the *Bridgewater* to come round to leeward of the reef where it would be possible to transfer the crew aboard her. He hoisted up an oar on which he tied two handkerchiefs, but by 10 o'clock the *Bridgewater* was seen to tack and was not seen again. Whether her captain saw the wrecks or the signal will never be known.

Therefore by midday casks of flour, beef, pork, water and spirits were being landed and the crew of the *Cato*, which was in a far worse state, swam through the surf, clinging to wreckage and were taken on board the *Porpoise*, although three young men were missing and must have drowned. As the tide receded more and more provisions and clothing were taken to the sandbank. Some of the crew of the

Cato had no clothes and "Fowler clothed four or five of them in Lieutenants' uniforms and much promotion of a similar kind had also taken place amongst our own people". Blankets and greatcoats were shared and pieces of the wreck used as firewood, so that they could dry out in the warmth of a fire.

The fact was, however, that although from three accounts of the incident, morale remained good and the officers were trusted, ninety men were marooned on a remote and barren island which Samuel Smith described as "a Small Uncertainty a hundred and fifty miles from the nearest land and upwards of nine hundred miles from the Nearest Port". Although concealing it the men on the reef must have had feelings of despair. In an account written in Calcutta some six months later, the Commander of the *Bridgewater* said, having drifted out of sight because of contrary winds he was too apprehensive to go back. Nevertheless, he was not far away and the ship was sighted and had not made the slightest effort to lower a boat either at dawn or when he must have seen the ships on the reef as he passed in the distance. Much good it did him, as although he reached Bombay his ship later disappeared on the way back to England and was presumed wrecked.

After a night safely on land of a sort, decisions had to be made about how to survive and to organise rescue and everyone had a task to perform. Tents were put up, a flagstaff raised to fly the distress signal: some went off fishing, seabirds' eggs were found and a quantity of sea spinach. The plant collection was gone but luckily it was only part of what had been gathered, the rest remaining at Port Jackson for a larger ship to take it to England where it was intended for Kew Gardens. Most of Westall's drawings were saved but a large number were damaged by sea water. Fortunately Flinders' papers survived, as otherwise all the work he had done would have been utterly wasted: the only papers missing were one or two he had been looking at when he heard the ghastly crash of timbers as the ship hit the reef.

Flinders as the senior officer had taken charge, calling the others together and putting forward a plan to organise a rescue. The largest cutter was to be repaired, equipped with oars and sail and made ready to return to Port Jackson to get help. The precious charts and journals were packed ready to retrieve them on return and Fowler was to be left in charge, with instructions that two other boats of sufficient size should be constructed, so that if Flinders had not returned within two months Fowler was to attempt to take off the survivors and get to Port Jackson. Taking Park, the commander of the *Cato*, and twelve men with him in the cutter which they named the *Hope*, Flinders left the reef on 26th August to loud cheers of those staying behind.

> An ensign with the union downward, had hitherto been kept hoisted as a signal to captain Palmer of our distress: but in the moment of enthusiasm a seaman quitted the crowd, and having obtained permission, ran to the flag staff, hauled down the ensign, and rehoisted it with the union in the upper canton. This symbolical expression of contempt for the *Bridgewater* and of confidence in the success of the voyage, I did not see without lively emotions.

Bligh's great navigational feat in a similar boat must have been in their minds, particularly as the winds were unfavourable, and they were to have some anxious moments.

Four days out they saw Cape Moreton and there landed to collect water, meeting a party of natives who were happy to help and who performed a dance for them. Turning south and after seven days and nights of continuous rowing they landed at a sheltered place for a night's sleep ashore, finding a supply of oysters, and two days later they arrived at Sydney Heads, having taken just two weeks to make the nine hundred mile voyage. In his book Flinders makes clear the relief they felt that those on Wreck Reef now had a chance of rescue.

Unshaven and dishevelled Flinders and Park walked up the hill to Government House, to find Governor King having dinner with his family. Describing the scene years later in his book he wrote:

> A razor had not passed over our faces from the time of the shipwreck, and the surprise of the Governor was not little at seeing two persons thus appear whom he supposed to be many hundred leagues on their way to England; but so soon as he was convinced of the truth of the vision before him, and learned the melancholy cause, an involuntary tear started from the eye of friendship and compassion, and we were received in the most affectionate manner.

For the colony with its limited resources, it was not an easy task to effect the rescue of 78 men left stranded on what came to be called Wreck Reef and to get them back to England together with the men who had been the crew of the cutter the *Hope*. Governor King immediately ordered the colonial schooner the *Francis* to prepare to sail and bring back to Sydney those men willing to return there. Fortunately the merchant ship the *Rolla* was about to leave for China with the intention of going on to India and her commander agreed to pick up any who would wish to make their way home by such a roundabout route. For Flinders himself it was thought that this would take far too long, as both he and King were anxious that he should get to England without such inordinate delay.

Therefore, he was to take the schooner the *Cumberland*, pick his crew and return direct to London. Flinders did have doubts, describing the schooner "as something less than a Gravesend passage boat, being only a burthen of twenty-nine tons", but he would be able to return by way of the Torres Strait which had been his original intention A further problem was that the *Cumberland* was somewhere up the Hawkesbury river. After waiting some days for her to come back Flinders in desperation took the *Hope* up the river to find her. She was brought back and quickly loaded with stores, some wine and food being donated by residents of Sydney, and the three ships left on 21st September, Flinders sailing out for the last time from the magnificent harbour that he knew so well.

Good progress was made in the first week although Flinders complained "that of all the filthy little things I ever saw, this schooner, for bugs, lice, fleas, weevils, mosquitoes, cockroaches (large and small), and mice, rises superior to them all". Nor was he impressed by the fact she admitted a lot of water for which the pumps were inadequate. Determined as he was to reach the Reef, he nevertheless "did not think favourably of the vessel in which I had undertaken a voyage half round the globe". The wind changed and only about fifty miles a day was achieved so that it was not until 7th October that they reached the reef. Fowler was out at sea testing the newly built boat and he was becoming concerned that no rescue ship had arrived when the sails of the *Rolla* were seen on the horizon. Soon the ships were seen from the reef where Samuel Flinders had been left as officer in charge. He was in a tent calculating lunar distances. On being told that the sails of three ships were in sight, Samuel replied that he supposed it was his brother coming back and asked to be told when the ships reached an anchorage and then calmly continued with his calculations. When the ships anchored he ordered a salute to be fired and joined in the general celebrations. There was one who was especially pleased to see his master. Trim, rescued from the wreck, had been well fed on fresh fish, but no doubt with loud mewing he made it quite clear that a reef was a pretty dull place for an adventurous cat to have to spend more than six weeks and he was taken on board the *Cumberland* where he would have made short work of the mice.

On the voyage Flinders had made decisions as to how the survivors should be divided up. He would take Aken, the Master of the *Investigator*, and eleven others, if they wished to go with him, and only one of them chose not to do so. In spite of the unsatisfactory state of the *Cumberland* he was determined to go on, at least as far as some port where a passage might be found in a better vessel, rather than waste time by turning back to Port Jackson, and Governor King had given him permission to do this if necessary. Fowler, Franklin and young Flinders were to take passage to Canton, and it is known that Samuel Smith went with them, and then make their way home, together with some of the others. The rest chose to go back to Sydney and within three days the ships parted company. Varying his course slightly from that made in the *Investigator* Flinders made his way through the Torres Strait and round to the Gulf of Carpentaria arriving at Kupang by 10th November where little had changed since the *Investigator's* call in March. Some fresh water was taken aboard but no pitch was obtainable to mend the leaks which were causing concern, nor was there hope of mending one of the pumps which was proving ineffective. With the monsoon likely to begin it was decided to press on as quickly as possible heading for the Cape of Good Hope, but unfortunate winds and thunder storms hampered progress.

Flinders was in a dilemma. The small size and the condition of the ship made it seem that it would be prudent to put in to port as soon as possible and see if there would be a possibility of getting another ship to continue the voyage back to London. At Port Jackson long discussions had taken place with Governor King who was inclined to think that Mauritius should be avoided, partly because so little was known of the unpredictable weather pattern in that area in November and December, although he had given Flinders a letter to the Governor, General Magallon.

The problem was that under the terms of the Peace of Amiens the Dutch were in control of the Cape of Good Hope and although the Governor might be friendly Flinders had no Dutch passport. His ship was unlikely to remain seaworthy rounding South Africa and continuing to St. Helena, the nearest British possession. On the other hand he was carrying a French passport and he hoped that even if Baudin was not in Mauritius, he must have called there and the Governor would have had a full report about the good reception he had been given at Port Jackson. A further difficulty was the rolling sea which was making it easier to head towards Mauritius.

As always Flinders picked up his quill pen and paper. A French trader had reported that during the months of November and December gusts of wind and bad weather prevailed in the area.

> On considering that the reporter might have an interest in keeping the Port Jackson people ignorant of the first prices of the goods which he had bought and might in future bring to sell them; and that the deviation from our course to the Cape was no more than 200 miles, I determined to put in at the isle Mauritius.

He went on to write:

> The upper works of the schooner had become so leaky
> as to require a spell from five to ten minutes in every
> hour to keep her free at this time; and as our pump geer
> is getting bad, being partly worn out, it was to be feared
> that if we should meet any unfavourable wind off the
> Cape to raise much sea and make the schooner heel,
> that we should hardly get round safe. One principal
> reason, therefore, for touching at Mauritius is to get
> the upper works caulked.

He continued that his main reason was the possibility
of finding a homeward bound ship which might make a
more expeditious passage than the little *Cumberland* whose
greatest rate of sailing was 7 knots and whose cramped
conditions made it almost impossible to do more than
write the daily log. He also thought that there were some
lesser reasons such as delivering Governor King's letters to
General Magallon which would otherwise have had to have
been sent from the Cape, and he would like to learn news
of *Le Géographe* and *Le Naturaliste*. And then followed
the sentence which contributed much to the troubles that
were to follow.

> Acquiring a knowledge of the periodical winds and
> weather there; of the port and the present state of
> the French colony; and how far it or its dependencies
> in Madagascar may be useful to Port Jackson; and
> also whether it may not be a convenient place for me
> to touch at during some part of my future expected
> voyage.

On the evening of 6th December he altered course, as he
put it "to the satisfaction of the people".

9

Your Excellency's Prisoner

A decision made, Flinders would have felt it was the right one and that he would receive a friendly reception, but care needed to be taken in approaching the unknown coast of the Île de France, as Mauritius[1] was known. He had no reason to suspect that these were to be the last hours that he would ever command a ship. He and one or two others were suffering from what he called a "bilious remitting fever" which he thought was caused by the wet and sultry weather which had meant that it was difficult to keep the ship well aired and clean. Given the conditions at Kupang, it is possible that the water taken on there again carried infection. With no medical officer on board, it was an additional reason for calling at a place where advice could be sought.

With a fair wind and no untoward incidents they made good time. Seeing a ship in the distance on the evening of 9th December, they headed towards her, and as dusk fell the *Cumberland* showed a light, but with full sail set the other ship seemed to be wishing to avoid them, sailing westwards and was lost to view.

At daybreak on 15th December the coast of the Île de France came in sight and at 11.30 a.m. a small schooner showing French colours came towards them, but then

---

[1] Named by the Dutch after Maurice, Prince of Orange in 1598: became French in 1715 and re-named Île de France: ceded to the British in 1814 when original name was restored.

veered off along the coast towards the Baie du Cap, where the crew were seen unloading hastily and running up the steep hill carrying muskets. It was Flinders' intention to ask for information about the way to approach the island's main harbour, Port Louis, or Port Nord-Ouest, as it was now called, but when contact was made he was told that the fragile Peace of Amiens was ended and that a state of war existed again between Britain and France. Furthermore, the French, with the Dutch, were in control of the Cape of Good Hope.

Flinders began to wonder if his passport, made out to him in 1801 as Commander of the *Investigator* would be accepted and when the local Commandant came on board with some other officers, he examined it carefully before saying that it must be sent to the Governor for inspection. It would have been unwise to part with the passport, but the Commandant suggested that an escort should be provided for Flinders to ride to Port Louis and that a pilot should then take the *Cumberland* round. Nevertheless, Flinders was troubled by the news of war and he seriously considered asking for a supply of fresh water and firewood and then attempting a dash to the Cape of Good Hope, but having learnt the French were there and knowing he could not possibly get as far as St. Helena without repairs to the ship, he had to abandon that idea. Flinders was invited ashore to dine with the French officers and some of the civilian residents by which time it was agreed that he should remain on board, taking a pilot with him to guide him to Port Louis. His hosts, accompanied by their wives, came to bid him farewell and brought with them a quantity of fruit and other food.

As the *Cumberland* anchored at Port Louis, Flinders may still have felt apprehensive, but bearing in mind that Cook and Vancouver had been received with courtesy, albeit long ago, and that much more recently Baudin had had an immense amount of help at Port Jackson at a time when France and England were thought to be at war, he appears not to have been too greatly concerned. He was to learn however, that General Magallon, to whom his letter from Governor King was addressed, had been replaced by an ardent Bonapartist, a friend of Napoleon and a former intelligence officer — General Charles Isodore De Caen.

Some knowledge of the events of the time and of De Caen's background helps to explain how his mind worked. Born at Caen in Normandy, he qualified as a lawyer before feeling he must serve his country by joining the Army in 1792 and as a captain in the Rhine Army his bravery on the battlefield was recognised. He was promoted to a General de Brigade, became an intelligence officer which brought him to the notice of Napoleon who was to regard him as a friend.

When Napoleon asked him to go to India as Governor to maintain French interests in the whole area of the Indian Ocean, he accepted and was promoted to the rank of Capitaine General (equivalent to Field Marshal). Admiral Comte Durand de Linois was also ordered to take his squadron to India, but under the command of De Caen, who, aged thirty four, was becoming arrogant, whereas de Linois was of a more chivalrous nature and they soon developed a hearty contempt of each other.

Under the terms of the Peace of Amiens the French possessions in India were to be restored to them, but when they reached Pondicherry the news had come through that the Treaty had been revoked and the British Governor refused to hand over power. De Caen had to withdraw to the Île de France, where he marched his soldiers to the military base and without having the courtesy to call on the island's Colonial Assembly issued orders to assert his authority. He sent de Linois off to Batavia and General Magallon, then the Governor, to Bourbon (now Réunion) to act as his deputy. Within a short time De Caen's despotic behaviour alienated the local population.

***

In full dress uniform in the steamy heat of the late afternoon in the hot season of the year, Flinders walked to Government House, accompanied by an officer and an interpreter, to be told that His Excellency the Captain General was having dinner and was not to be interrupted. He was allowed to sit in a shady place where he was joined by some French officers who spoke English. They asked if he had really come from Port Jackson in such a small vessel and also about Baudin's stay there and the voyage of Monsieur Flinedare, "of which to their surprise I knew nothing, but afterwards found it to be my own name which they so pronounced". Two hours passed waiting, and then another half hour whilst De Caen discussed the matter with officials before Flinders was shown in to meet "a shortish thick man in a laced round jacket and the other a genteel-looking man whose blood seemed to circulate more tranquilly".

De Caen, without the slightest preliminary politeness, demanded both the passport and commission, firing off a list of questions. It may be understandable that he found it hard to believe that the Governor of New South Wales had allowed a twenty-nine ton vessel to be taken from Port Jackson to Mauritius, with the intention of going on to England. He could not see how this extraordinary and what he thought was a foolhardy voyage should be undertaken for the purpose of returning home to get another ship to bring out to continue discovery. He demanded further papers and to know why the *Cumberland* had put into Mauritius and Flinders, through the interpreter, tried to explain that it was necessity that had caused him to stop in passing. "At this answer the general lost the small share of patience of which he seemed to be possessed, and said with much gesture and an elevated voice 'You are imposing on me'."

Dismissing him abruptly, De Caen demanded that all papers aboard the *Cumberland* were to be produced and sent his officers to the ship to see that they were packed into a trunk and brought ashore. At one o'clock in the morning Flinders and the Master, Aken, were ordered ashore under arrest. They were allowed to pack some clothes and taking Trim with them they were marched to the Café Marengo for what was said to be a few days. It was a dirty cheap establishment with an upper floor which could be guarded: the two rooms into which they were put had a pair of truckle beds and were full of both mosquitoes and bugs. At dawn two sentries arrived: one stood outside whilst the other paced up and down the rooms, but Flinders records that a good breakfast and dinner were served.

Flinders was sent for again and interviewed by the Governor's secretary who was a German, but spoke some English. More questions were fired. De Caen had refused to believe the explanation of either the poor state of the *Investigator* or the shipwreck of the *Porpoise* and he may have thought Governor King's letter was a forgery. He was accusing Flinders of chasing a ship into the Baie du Cap and wanted to know on whose authority he had come to Port Louis. All the questions and answers were written down before Flinders was sent back to the Café Marengo.

Surprisingly, a servant was sent later in the day with an invitation to dine with De Caen. Flinders, apart from being angry and insulted at being called to all intents a liar, refused the invitation, saying he had already dined, which he had, but added that when he was at liberty if His Excellency thought proper to invite him he would be flattered to accept. Some French officers visited to ask him to change his mind, but he would not do so feeling he had been grossly insulted and may well have thought it was a trick to ply him with wine to make him talk in such a way as to implicate him as a spy. In any case, was he really to be taken to dine formally and then be returned to that hot and dirty room?

We shall never know if De Caen meant to apologise, but he regarded the refusal as an insult to his wife. Many have said that Flinders should have accepted, but it should be remembered that it was not just the short term fever from which Flinders was suffering. Apart from the fact that he had already dined, the events of the last two and a half years had taken their toll. He was a man exhausted and in despair: possibly this affected his judgment as he was to say himself in *"The Voyage to Terra Australis"*. Nowadays he might well have been ordered to hospital and offered counselling. As it was De Caen did send an officer to say he would be invited to dine when he was at liberty, but no explanation of his arrest was given.

The following day there was a further demand to attend at Government House, but on arrival Flinders was told that the General could not see him and that the trunk full of papers was being opened. In it were not only the despatches with which Governor King had entrusted him, but his journal written a few days before containing the sentence about the winds and weather and the present state of the French colony. De Caen seems to have exploded. All the charts and accounts of exploration, all the knowledge he had of the help and hospitality given to Baudin were to count as nothing, nor the fact that when Flinders left Port Jackson he had no knowledge that war had broken out again. De Caen was convinced that Flinders had arrived with an unlikely story, that his papers were merely a cover and that his real purpose was to find out something of the defences of the island, which were in fact in a weak state. De Caen was probably in fear of Napoleon who had charged him with the defence of the area and whilst his role was to watch the interests of France, he saw himself as the man who would bring that part of the world under French domination, drawing up plans to invade India and sending his brother home to present those plans to Napoleon.

Apart from De Caen's intense dislike of the English, matters were made much worse for Flinders by François Péron, the most senior naturalist aboard *Le Géographe*. He had very recently written a very long "mémoire politique" addressed to De Caen alleging, quite wrongly, that the English intended to use Port Jackson as a base from which to attack South America and that Flinders was probably on his way to spy out the coastline. He also said that the English were likely to attack the French possessions in the Indian Ocean. Flinders' arrival must, therefore, have made De Caen think that he was indeed there to assess the defences.

It is an interesting document historically as in it Péron describes Sydney as it was at that time, but it starts with a statement that the French expedition had not been made principally to gather botanical specimens, but had been a device to fool the British Government into granting a passport so that the French could assess what was happening. (The question might be asked whether Baudin, being above all a naturalist and a serious collector of plants, was naïve enough not to understand this.)

Péron continued by recalling his time at Port Jackson when as a scientist he was able to ask many questions which would have been indiscreet for others to ask, and that he had been received by the Governor on a number of occasions. However, it was Colonel Paterson, the Deputy Governor, who he described as a *savant* and a member of the Royal Society of London, who was especially helpful, receiving him into his house, treating him like a son and accompanying him on long excursions into the interior of the country.

Far from being a small colony struggling at Botany Bay, which is described as a humid, marshy and sterile place with poor anchorage, Port Jackson's harbour was superb and although the soil there was sandy, further inland many farms and settlements were being established in very fertile country, with fine roads and houses being built.

Colonists were encouraged to come from England by being given financial help for the voyage with allowances made for families. On arrival they were granted land and a number of convicts would be drafted to help work it. A house would be built, furniture and clothes provided, together with tools, seed and farm animals.

For the first eighteen months the settlers would receive a ration of food and for the first five years no tax would be levied. After that a small tax was to be paid, increasing annually. Then a comment is made on the wisdom of the English. If a settler had been noticeably hard working and successful, he would be offered more land without payment and his liability to tax would be deferred.

Péron described how the different types of cattle and sheep were thriving remarkably well and forecast that before long the colony would be supplying materials for manufacture in England. He mentioned mineral deposits and also said that French *vignerons* were being employed and vines were being imported from Madeira and the Cape.

All this meant that the colony would expand, settlements would be made along the coast and in Van Diemen's Land over the Bass Strait.

The document finished with a recommendation that Sydney should be destroyed and wrote that Lieutenant Louis de Freycinet had taken particular note of places where troops might be landed.

Whilst he openly despised Baudin, blaming him for slow progress, Péron's personal antagonism towards Flinders arose because his discoveries had been successful, whereas the French had failed. Although when he wrote he could not have realised that Flinders was to appear asking for assistance, nevertheless his report must have influenced De Caen and been a major factor in the decision to keep Flinders a prisoner.

De Caen had questioned at the beginning whether the man calling himself Matthew Flinders was the real Flinders or an impostor sent in to spy. Baudin, who would have recognised him had died at Mauritius on 16th September 1803, and his two ships had sailed for France only a few days before the arrival of the *Cumberland*. Some of the crew had stayed in Mauritius, but no attempt seems to have been made to identify Flinders. Impostor or not De Caen was convinced that he was dangerous: he was not a man to change his mind.

Flinders wrote a letter to him attempting to explain at length that he had not violated his passport by putting into the port to acquire a knowledge of the periodical winds or the state of the colony.

Nothing can in my opinion, add to the propriety of the intention with which I put into the port, but I shall justify it by the example of your own nation; and to do so it is only necessary for me to refer to the instructions of the published voyage of the unfortunate La Pérouse.[2]

Your Excellency will there see, that the most lamented navigator was ordered to make particular observations upon the trade, situation of every port where he might touch; so that if the example of your own nation be taken as a standard of propriety, the plea for making me a prisoner is altogether untenable.

He went on to say that the two captains, Baudin and Hamelin were not forbidden to make remarks about the state of the English colony in spite of the fact that it was believed that France and England were at war, and no demands were ever made to see their journals. He appealed to De Caen as "the representative of a great nation which has hitherto shown itself forward to protect and encourage those sciences by which knowledge of mankind is forwarded" and pointed out that his patron was Sir Joseph Banks, known in France and throughout the literary world, who had charged him to retrace part of the voyage of Captain Cook.

He then set out the story of the decayed state of the *Investigator*, of the shipwreck and how he was given the *Cumberland*, which he described as a small schooner of 29 tons, a mere boat, in order to reach England, repeating that it was necessity that caused him to call at Mauritius.

Now, Sir, I would beg to ask you whether it becomes the

---

[2] La Pérouse had put into Sydney Cove a few days after the arrival of the First Fleet in 1788 and received assistance. After his departure he was not heard of again and was believed wrecked on the Barrier Reef. Flinders had spent time looking for any sign of the wreck.

French nation, independently of all passport, to stop the progress of such a voyage, of which the whole maritime world are to receive the benefit. How contrary to this was her conduct some years since towards Captain Cook. But the world highly applauded her conduct then, and possibly we may sometime see what the general sentiment will be in the present case.

I sought protection and assistance in your Port and I have found a Prison.

Judge for me as a man, Sir, judge for me as a British officer employed in a neutral expedition, judge for me as a zealous philanthropist, what I feel at being thus treated. At present I quit the subject with the following requests: that I may be permitted to have my printed books on shore and that my servant may be allowed to attend in my apartment.

With all the respect due from my situation to the Capt. Gl. I am your Excellency's obedient servant.

De Caen was implacable and a modern translation of his reply reads:-

De Caen, Commanding Officer, French Naval Bases, to the East of the Cape of Good Hope to Captain Flinders, Commander of the schooner *Cumberland*:

I had made no response to your letter of 21.X[3], Captain, because it was becoming pointless for us to engage ourselves in a discussion on my conscious decision, justifiable or not, to retain the *Cumberland*, until I received fresh orders.

In addition, I would have had too much of an advantage in being able to refute your assertions despite their being so heavily laced with reasonings and examples.

I would much have preferred to ascribe the somewhat

---

[3] Dated according to new calendar of the French.

intemperate tone of this letter to an ill-humour in which your current situation has put you. I have thought for some time that, having given serious consideration to the causes and the circumstances, you would also accord yourself such a period of restrained silence, to draw even further away but your last letter leaves me no alternative. Your enterprise, as extraordinary as ill-conceived, to leave Port Jackson in the *Cumberland*, more to demonstrate an unofficial zeal for the individual interests of Great Britain, than for that which the French Government was persuaded to grant you a passport, and which I shall expand on at another time and place, had already conveyed to me some idea of your character; but this letter, exceeding all bounds of decency, compels me to tell you until general opinion may judge the tone of your letters or mine, to cease all correspondence that aims to demonstrate the justice of your cause, since you give little indication of any ability to observe the rules of etiquette.

Je vous salus

De Caen

Flinders was allowed to go to Government House to collect some of his books, papers and chests, when he found the third volume of his journal, with its entry written on approaching Mauritius, had been confiscated. He never saw it again and was not until some sixty years later that the British Government was able to persuade the French to hand it over to them. On New Year's Day 1804, Flinders started work on checking his charts of the Gulf of Carpentara, where he had been exactly a year before.

Elder, his boatswain, was allowed to come ashore to act as his servant. Flinders also asked to be able to write letters home and was told that he might write to whom he pleased, provided they were seen by the Town Marshal before despatch, which made him realise with what suspicion he was regarded. Letters were written to the Admiralty and to Sir Joseph Banks, who in turn wrote to Monsieur Delambre, a distinguished French astronomer, hoping he would ask the Institut National to take up the matter, but with the difficulties of postal services between two countries at war it was months before a reply was received from Delambre to say that the Institut agreed to do so. The case of Captain Flinders was to become a *cause célèbre*, particularly amongst scientists and literary men, both in Paris and London because it was always understood that war should not stand in the way of advancement of knowledge.

On 3rd February another approach was made to the Governor, once more proposing that he should be allowed to depart with his papers and charts when

> I will pledge my honour not to give any information of the Île de France or anything belonging to it, for a limited time, if it be thought that I have gained any information, or if judged necessary any other restrictions can be laid upon me.
>
> 2nd If this will not be complied with I request to be sent to France.
>
> 3rd But if it is indispensable to detain me here, I request that my officer (Aken) and people be permitted to depart in the schooner; as well as for the purpose of informing the British Admiralty where I am, as to relieve our families and friends from the report which will be spread of the total loss of the *Porpoise* and the *Cato*.

He went on to say that whatever restrictions necessary could be placed on Aken and then signed himself

"Your Excellency's prisoner".

De Caen took no notice.

Flinders did not know that in the meantime De Caen had written to Denis Decrès, the Minister of Marine and the Colonies in Paris to ask what should be done about this prisoner who was considered dangerous. Therefore, he could not release him on his own authority, even if inclined to do so, particularly as it was likely that Napoleon himself would hear about it.

Concerned about the crew left aboard the *Cumberland*, Flinders paid for vegetables to be sent to them from the market, but Aken, who was allowed out fairly frequently, reported that not only was the ship showing signs of deterioration, but that the men had broken into the Captain's cupboard, found brandy and had got drunk. On 23rd March they were taken off the ship and sent to a prison on the other side of the island. This meant that their captain would no longer subsidise their food, which he could ill afford to do, as by then he was running out of money to the point where he could not afford to have his clothes laundered. The only means of getting money was by bills drawn on London when 30% was taken off from the transaction. It was later reported that the men were being badly treated, being given only one meal a day, and that very inadequate, and that they had not been allowed to take sufficient clothes with them. Following a complaint to De Caen this was investigated and put right, although rather tardily, and eventually they were allowed to return to England.

***

Flinders continued to be guarded closely although an interpreter was allowed to visit him and two members of De Caen's staff named Colonel Monistrol and Captain Bergeret, who treated him with courtesy. Jacques Bergeret had been a prisoner of war in England, but on release had gone to Mauritius. During an action in the Indian Ocean he had captured three English merchant ships. Two of the captains had their wives with them and on bringing them to Mauritius he had insisted that they were all properly housed and well treated. He was to visit Flinders many times and was unfailingly helpful. Flinders received frequent visits from a surgeon who ordered a diet of vegetables and lemon juice to counteract the effects of scurvy from which he still suffered. As early as January the surgeon had said that he must be moved to better quarters but it was not until 31st March that he was moved to La Maison Despaux, known as the Garden Prison, which was used to detain officer prisoners of war. He had spent his 30th birthday at the Café Marengo and for a man who had always been active, it was a hard punishment to have been kept in a hot depressing mosquito ridden room, only allowed out on the roof at night to take some air.

With Aken he was allowed to choose two rooms, and another one for their two servants. The garden was a rough area, with muddy paths running through grass, but had a number of fruit trees and at least it provided space. It would seem a place which Trim would enjoy, but there must have been a difficulty in letting him in and out of the house, Flinders being concerned at the surly attitude of the guards, and so with reluctance he accepted the offer of a kindly French woman who said he would make a companion for her young daughter. Within a fortnight Trim disappeared and in spite of offers of a reward he was not seen again. He had been such a wonderful friend and companion that Flinders felt his loss deeply, but with a cat of such adventurous spirit it was perhaps inevitable that he would meet a sticky end.

Whilst Flinders was at the Café Marengo, De Caen had not asked for his sword to be handed over, which inferred that he was not technically a prisoner of war, but on the 2nd June a sergeant arrived at the Garden Prison to demand it. Flinders insisted that proper protocol should be observed and asked that an officer of equal rank should call, when the sword would be surrendered and in this he was supported by the commander of the prison. Nothing happened until September, when an officer, although of lower rank, called and Flinders gave up his sword.

To have more space and to have company helped, but the talk would have been endlessly about the possibility of being part of an exchange of prisoners of war. This was organised by allowing prisoners to board unarmed and neutral merchant ships, known as cartels, which were bound for ports in countries such as India, South Africa or even America, from where a further passage might be arranged to get them home. The same system applied to letters.

What of letters to Ann? Like her when the *Investigator* had sailed from England, it seems that in his unhappiness he could not bring himself to write to her direct. He did write, however, two letters to her step-father perhaps feeling that he would break the news to her gently, and at least these meant that she took off the mourning clothes which she had worn on hearing the rumour that the *Cato* and the *Porpoise* were lost with all on board. It may be, also, that he felt he could not write a letter expressing his feelings which would be read by the Town Marshal, and it was some months before he had the heart to do so.

August 24th 1804

I yesterday enjoyed a delicious piece of misery in reading over thy dear letters, my beloved Ann. Shall I tell thee that I have never before done it since I have been shut up in this prison. The first day of January I dedicated to 'the pleasures of misery' and was violently tempted to go further, but I rushed into something else and escaped a further addition to the misery of recollection. ....

I have many friends, who are kind and much interested for me, and I certainly love them, but yet before thee they disappear as stars before the rays of the morning sun. I cannot connect the idea of happiness with anything but thee. Without thee, the world would be a blank.

He continues by saying that he is distressed about the accounts of the state of her eyes and her health and hopes that the attacks have not returned since the letter to him was written from Boston in September 1802. He describes the large house and wishes she could be there, saying that she would not lack female company as there were two ladies held as prisoners, living in a house about four miles away.

I am not without friends even among the French. On the contrary, I have several, and but one enemy, unfortunately the last, is all-powerful here; nor will he on any persuasion permit me to pass the walls of the prison, although some others who are thought less dangerous have had that indulgence occasionally.

He talks of his return to London and hopes that no further misfortune will prevent them meeting.

Indeed my Ann, thou knowest not how very dear thou art to me. At the same time I respect and reverence thy very superior qualifications. I love thee most tenderly. ..... miserably torn asunder as we have indeed been but we shall reunite, never perhaps to be separated, and our second marriage shall be more delightful than the first.

After suggesting that she should "buy a little horse, my love and take the air as often as thou canst" he hopes that they will spend some time together in the country visiting their friends and there follows an amusing message to Belle, Ann's half-sister.

> Health, my dearest love, most anxiously do I wish thee. This is now a fine season in England. May thou be now happy in the enjoyment of it.
>
> Thy most affectionate
>
> Matth^w Flinders.

Concerned about Ann's well-being, he did not mention his own health, but on 29th September he wrote in his journal that he was not positively ill, but not well enough to follow his pursuits, arising in part, probably, from a depression of spirits. Pains in the legs, swellings in the glands of the neck, dimness of sight and headache, were sufficient to produce a depression of spirits.

A number of French residents of Port Louis began to call at the Garden Prison, including Thomas Pitot (often known as Thomi) and his brother Edouard, and occasionally they dined there. The Pitot family had lived in Mauritius for some time, but had returned to France in 1792. When their father died the two boys continued their education there, but the revolutionary government was to take away all their money and send them to the Bastille. On their release they joined other French aristocrats in England for two years before going back to Mauritius and setting up a trading company owning several ships. Thomas Pitot spoke English, was widely read and as he had a collection of English books, he lent them to Flinders, together with some musical scores, which helped to increase his repertoire when playing his flute.

Accompanied by his interpreter, Flinders was allowed to dine with the Danish Consul, who was helpful in cashing bills at par, and there was also an occasion when some

French officers took four of the prisoners to the theatre. Unfortunately the theatre was crammed and they could hardly see the stage, and although by that time Flinders had learnt some basic French, he cannot have understood a great deal. However, it was a welcome change of scene and he made a comment in his journal about the expensive clothes of the women, mostly the wives and daughters of local tradesmen, who were far better dressed than women in England. The older women he described as fat, but that did not stop them displaying their bosoms in a similar manner to the younger ones and he thought that the sight of so many women so undressed would raise an uproar in an English theatre. "The prudes would break their fans, the aged would cry shame, the libertines would exalt and the old lechers would apply their opera glasses."

At one time he wrote that his health was "mawkish", but that this was to be expected in a man held prisoner. Except when he had trouble with his right eye, which he thought he must have strained by the constant use of his spy glass when at sea and now affected by indifferent health, he worked on his papers. When Aken, who suffered much ill health and had had to be admitted to hospital, was released and allowed to board a cartel, Flinders entrusted him with a number of documents, including the first map of the outline of Australia.

In a letter written to Ann on New Year's Eve 1804 he was able to say

> My health is much better here than I could have expected, considering the nature of the climate and my imprisonment; and my appetite is so good that I believe it has an intention of revenging me on the governor by occasioning a famine in the island.

Unfortunately, a few weeks later he was taken ill with what

he called the "constitutional gravely complaint" from which he had suffered some years before. This kidney complaint was to recur, and it was to be the cause of his death in 1814.

By July 1805 all the prisoners at La Maison Despaux had been allowed to leave and as the surgeon who visited quite frequently had been urging that Flinders should be moved to live up in the hills he wrote to De Caen on 17th August asking if he might move to the plantation house of Madame D'Arifat at Wilhems Plains, an arrangement that had been negotiated by Thomas Pitot. On the 22nd he signed a parole agreeing not to move more than nine miles from the plantation and to conduct himself "with that proper degree of reserve, becoming an officer residing in a country with which his nation is at war."

10

Le Refuge

Thomas Pitot meanwhile had been preparing a celebration, and immediately on his release he took Flinders to his house in the town for tea, and together they went to thank Captain Bergeret who had done so much to set up the parole. The following day, having cleared the official business, Pitot arranged a grand musical evening followed by supper at the house of Monsieur and Madame Deglos. Being the guest of honour Flinders had to escort Madame Deglos to the table, which with his limited French and having for so long been unused to elegant society, he found overwhelming.

Early next morning Edouard Pitot, Thomas' brother, took Flinders out to climb La Pauce mountain. In his rather weakened state perhaps it was as well that it rained heavily and they were unable to reach the top, but with umbrellas open they got half way, where they ate breakfast. In the afternoon there was another party at the Pitots' house, where he was introduced to Monsieur and Madame de Chazal who were to become his very good friends as they were neighbours of Madame D'Arifat. In the evening there was a visit to the theatre.

The next day, breakfast was taken at Madame Deglos' house, followed by a round of visits and finally a meeting with Madame D'Arifat who, with her daughters, was staying in Port Louis waiting for her eldest son to return from the neighbouring island of Bourbon.

Leaving at 4.0 o'clock the following afternoon the Pitots took their guest to their country home about five miles out of the town and next morning before breakfast arranged a shooting expedition. Then the journey continued on donkeys, stopping on the way at Le Reduit, the large government country house that was being repaired for the use of the Governor. The night was spent at another plantation house, Flinders remarking on the generous hospitality received: it was not until 4 o'clock the following afternoon that their hosts allowed them to leave.

It got dark and the rain came down again, so shelter was sought at the country house of the de Chazals and the next day they reached Le Refuge where Flinders chose to make a home in a small pavilion with a similar one for his two servants, feeling that he did not wish to intrude upon the family. After the long months in prison he was exhausted by struggling with French conversation and overwhelmed by the hospitality he had received. Before leaving, Pitot, anxious to ensure that Flinders was not isolated, introduced him to Madame Couve, whose husband's plantation bordered on that of the D'Arifats. She invited him to call at any time, to the delight of her two very musical young daughters. This open invitation was accepted a few days later, the first of many visits, where encountering Monsieur Murat, a retired commander in the merchant marine he invited him to dine. Murat spoke no English, but Flinders saw him as a chance to improve his conversational French and he became a frequent visitor. Enjoying his new found freedom, Flinders explored the hills and woods, sometimes taking Elder with him on shooting forays. Gradually recovering his health to a great extent, he began writing very detailed descriptions of the surrounding country, its climate and geology.

On 21st October Pitot took him to see the great cascades

on the Rivière du Tamarin. Whilst Pitot was looking at
the views from the top, Flinders descended to a cave
where the water projected over it at some distance, and
made some notes about the formation of the falls. Then
sitting there he

> passed to the vicissitudes of my own life. I was born
> in the fens of Lincolnshire where a hill is not to be
> seen for many miles, at a distance from the sea, and
> my family unconnected with sea affairs of any kind
> of enterprise or ambition. After many incidents of
> fortune and adventure, I found myself a commander in
> the Royal Navy, having been charged with an arduous
> expedition of discovery; have visited a great variety of
> countries, made three times the tour of the world; find
> my name known in more kingdoms than that where I
> was born, with some degree of credit; and this moment
> a prisoner in a mountainous island in the Indian Ocean,
> lying under a cascade in a situation very romantic and
> interior, meditating upon the progress which nature
> is continually making towards a moderate degree
> of equality in the physical and moral worlds; and in
> company with a foreigner, a Frenchman whom I call,
> and believe to be, my friend.

The following day, whilst at the de Chazal's he received
a note from Pitot, enclosing letters which had arrived
which included one "from my beloved wife", others from
relations and one from Sir Joseph Banks which said that
he was corresponding with Ann and trying to reassure her.
He also said that there was a prospect of an order being
given for liberation, through representations made by the
Institut National in Paris. The news from Sir Joseph raised
his hopes, but it was to be one of the many false hopes
that he had of being liberated.

The six weeks before the D'Arifats returned gave him
time to recuperate, but when they invited him to live in

the house, he hesitated before asking if he might continue to live in the pavilion and to dine with the family each day, paying for his food as they were obviously not very well off. He was still finding it difficult to adjust, often glad when some social event finished so that he could return to his room, look at his books, play his flute and indulge in a little private melancholy as he called it over his frustration that he could not leave the island to return to London, not only to present his work to the Admiralty and have it published, but to see Ann again.

The D'Arifats were a well educated family with a group of friends who were members of the Societé d'Emulation, meeting frequently for discussion and subscribing to a number of journals sent out from Paris which resulted in correspondence with the Institut National. Mainly planters and merchants in Mauritius, their interests were in literature, music and the new scientific developments. Surprise is sometimes expressed that people in far away places were so well informed, but it was not only at universities or in cathedral cities or in the capitals of Europe that there was interest in learning and the arts. In England many a country squire or a parson such as Mr. Shinglar at Horbling was widely read and in the long winter evenings gathered friends together or joined such groups as the Spalding Gentlemen's Society, which Dr. Johnson visited.

So it was in the Île de France. The kindness shown to Flinders was remarkable. France and England were at war, but that made no difference. There may at first have been a certain curiosity about this young captain who had circumnavigated the newly discovered land mass to the south, been shipwrecked and now detained indefinitely by the Governor who was so much disliked. But here was no ordinary sea dog, however brave or skilled, but a man of a brilliant and enquiring mind and the residents of the Île de France did all they could to draw him into their circle, to invite him to stay, to take him on shooting expeditions. Flinders was restricted to an area nine miles from Le Refuge, which meant he could not go into Port Louis without special permission, nor travel far across the island, but nevertheless he was received or visited by thirty nine different families. One result is that his diary gives us an idea of the life led by the planters and professional families of the island at that time.

The attractive wooden plantation houses with verandas and window shutters to keep out the heat were some distance apart, but the owners visited each other frequently, riding through the wooded hills to meet for dinner, conversation and musical evenings. Picnic parties were described and the men enjoyed shooting expeditions. A variety of crops was grown on the land worked by slaves. Those who were merchants had to spend more time in Port Louis, but some had country houses as well. In the cooler months of the year families might move down to Port Louis where they would be able to have contacts with people whose plantations were further away.

In replying to the letter he had received from Ann he wrote:

> Receive my best beloved, my thanks for your communication, but especially for thy sweet assurances of unaltered affection, and with them receive my vows of constant unabated love: to love thee more than I have done, and now do, I think cannot be, thou has the sole undivided possession of my heart.

The letter continues with a description of the D'Arifat family consisting of three sons and three daughters, adding that it is with the eldest son, aged about twenty seven and the daughter aged about twenty with whom he had become particularly friendly.

> Thou canst not conceive how anxious they are to see
> and be acquainted with thee. Tho unknown, I scarcely
> think that thou art less dear to Mademoiselle Delphine
> D'Arifat than to many of thy relations. She talks of
> making a voyage to England in the peace in order to see
> more of our English manners and to make acquaintance
> with thee.

Madame D'Arifat asked Flinders to give lessons in
mathematics to two of her sons and to teach English to
two of her daughters, who in turn would help Flinders to
learn French.

Delphine was a very pretty girl, possibly rather wilful.
With the rather restricted life she had led she had never
met anyone outside her immediate circle and unfortunately
she was at once attracted to the newcomer. That Flinders
found her attractive there is little doubt: he liked intelligent
women. He wrote in his diary:

> She is an extraordinary young lady, possessing a strength
> of mind, a resolution and a degree of penetration which
> few men can boast of …. 'Tis pity she had not been
> born a man, and in a more extensive field than the Isle
> of France.

Apart from lessons, they saw each other daily at meals, on
the excursions the family made, and they would have been
able to ride beside each other when going out to dine with
neighbours. It has been said they had an affair, but this is
unlikely as Madame D'Arifat would have been careful to
see that no scandal should attach to her daughter's name.
Being a widow of limited means, she would hope that her
daughter would marry suitably, and she knew that Flinders
had a wife in England. It was one thing for married women
to have affairs — they did — but quite another for young
girls. Flinders had the sense to dine out fairly often, but
nevertheless Delphine was sent off to stay with her elder

brother at Flacq, on the far side of the island, where she took her lessons with an Englishwoman married to a French resident. Delphine returned home and later a quarrel is recorded, she having been off-hand to the point of rudeness. However, they seem to have got over this and Delphine embroidered a purse to send to Ann.

A routine was established at Le Refuge. They rose early and Flinders took a bathe in a cool stream (describing it as "tolerably cool work"), before joining the family for a walk across the garden to let out the hens. After breakfast at 7.30 the lessons took place followed by Flinders working on his observations made during his voyage, in studying the geology of the area, in writing letters. It was the custom to dine at 2.0 p.m., often with neighbours, sometimes staying on to supper or even overnight if their conversations went on late or if there was heavy rain. Their days ended by 10.0 p.m. unless there was a special party.

Flinders did not much care for dancing, particularly the high vaulting style favoured by the French which he considered was not so graceful or as decent as the English style. Again he commented on the women's dress saying that whilst it might be delightful to behold, it was not what he could choose for women of his own family. One evening, accompanied by the elderly Monsieur Murat, he offered to escort home from the de Chazal's house, the two daughters of Madame Couve. This was not permitted, as they were afraid of the gossip that might follow, which was something Flinders found difficult to reconcile with their dancing so energetically showing quite so much flesh.

Whilst Pitot came to see Flinders every week except when he was away on business in Bourbon, he continued to help in every possible way, but it was with his nearer neighbours, the de Chazals, that he frequently dined and spent many musical evenings, Madame de Chazal being a talented pianist. It was not the custom to have a particular celebration at Christmas, but it was on Christmas Day 1806 that Flinders, invited to dinner, was asked by his host to sit for a portrait. Further sittings took place and the portrait was finished by the middle of January. The portrait shows Flinders as a man of determination, but there is a look of sadness in his eyes.[1]

New Year's Day was the time of celebration. The slaves presented the mistress of the house with nosegays and Flinders gave money to those slaves who had been of service to him. The slaves had a free day celebrating it with a party where most of them got drunk.

In the cooler months of the year it became very damp in the high country where Le Refuge was situated, so much so that Flinders had to take his clothes and papers over to the main house to air. The family moved down nearer the sea and Flinders was permitted to join them from time to time. He was only allowed occasional short visits to Port Louis — six in all, but he made two unauthorised ones. He stayed with the Pitots and met three officers who had served in *Le Géographe* and *Le Naturalist*, one of whom was Baudin's nephew, Charles.

As time went by Flinders became almost part of the D'Arifat family, and when in 1808 Lise, the youngest daughter was married to Charles Desbassyns, one of the wealthiest men in the two islands of Bourbon and the Île de France, he was not only invited to the wedding but signed the registers at both the church service and at the civil ceremony, and was told that if a son was born he would receive the name Flinders.

---

[1] This picture remained in the family until fairly recently and was in the home in Lincolnshire of one of de Chazal's descendants. It was then sold and is now in the Art Gallery of South Australia in Adelaide.

In spite of the kindness of his friends, Flinders grew
more and more frustrated. Elder, still acting as his
servant, became depressed too. Although Flinders tried
to teach him French, he found this too difficult and the
lack of communication with others made him fearful and
he became obsessed with the thought that everyone was
plotting against him. Flinders was so concerned that he
took him into his own pavilion for safety at night. With
his master dining out or going over to the main house so
regularly, Elder's duties must have been fairly light, but he
became reluctant to do the tasks asked of him. Flinders
gave Elder a letter to take to Port Louis asking that he
should be released and he went off quite cheerfully to
deliver it. The other men from the *Cumberland* including
one who had acted as the second servant, had already been
released, so there was no reason to hold Elder who had
volunteered to stay on. He was allowed to take passage on
a ship sailing for Baltimore, where he could get a further
passage home and Flinders gave him a present of $100.
Although relieved of the anxiety of caring for him, the
last link with the *Investigator* was broken.

News of the progress of the war reached Mauritius from
Paris and Flinders knew about the Battle of Trafalgar in
1805 and the death of William Pitt in 1806. Pitot did his
best to keep him informed and even gave him a copy of the
Navy List. In this there was a notice about the *Investigator*.
He wrote immediately to Ann asking her to find out what
this meant. Was this a new ship, or had the old *Investigator*
been patched up and taken home? Until his final return to
England he did not know, as he ceased to receive any letters
from home. Seemingly the difficulties of communications
from England had become insuperable.

It is hardly surprising therefore that Flinders had his times
of frustration and melancholy and increasingly felt his long

stay in the Île de France was a waste of valuable time. At least he knew that Aken had delivered to the Admiralty his earlier writings and a paper he had sent to Banks which had been read to members of the Royal Society in March 1806. Writing with a quill pen, he worked for hours collating, refining and copying his charts and above all working on the "Observations upon the marine barometer, made on board His Majesty's Ship *Investigator* during the examination of the coasts of New South Wales 1801, 1802, 1803," and his theory that the magnetism of the earth and the iron in a ship affected the ship's compass.

The work he did over his years in Mauritius is not widely understood, but it was to contribute significantly to the accuracy of coastal charts and the safety of navigation across the world. It was to lead to the general use of an upright bar placed on the binnacle and which after 1837 was known as the Flinders' Bar when the Admiralty became concerned about the effect upon compasses carried in iron clad ships. Nowadays modern main compasses are normally gyros, unaffected by magnetism, but all ships still carry an emergency magnetic compass fitted with the Flinders Bar.

The final page of his treatise is dated November 1809 when he wrote:

> I purpose, if it shall please God that I may be liberated from this imprisonment in the Isle of France, to take the first opportunity, of making all the necessary experiments for ascertaining the magnetism of ships as far as can be useful to the accuracy of navigation; as also of making such as may enable me to determine the points on the surface of the earth to which the needle of the compass is directed and also the places of the poles within the earth which affect the dipping needle; what I have done here being only preparatory to what

I propose to do hereafter, when I shall have been able
to collect proper materials.

From time to time Flinders wrote to Ann and in one letter
written on 19th March 1806 he mused that he wished it
were possible for her to join him if his stay in Mauritius
was to continue indefinitely, but realised that it would be
very difficult for her to travel to America and there find
a ship that would take her to Mauritius. He did not think
she should travel alone, as "let the conduct of a woman on
board a ship without her husband be ever so prudent and
circumspect, the tongue of slander will almost certainly
find occasion, or it will create one, to embitter the peace of
her husband and family." The journey could only be made
if she could find someone to escort her, if perhaps she was
acquainted with a captain of a ship or some respectable
man who had his wife with him.

Of all things in the world, I most desire thy presence
here, since I cannot come to thee: but of all things in the
world I should dread thy undertaking the voyage without
being protected and accommodated in a manner which
is scarcely possible any opportunity should place in thy
reach.

Nevertheless, some money was transferred to Ann's
stepfather in case such a chance arose. He also asked De
Caen if he had any objections and was told that provided
a passport was obtained from France he would have no
objections. Flinders later wrote that this request was made
partly to test if the Governor might say that there was no
point as release was imminent.

Over the years of his imprisonment many letters were
written about the prospect of his release. He wrote to
Joseph Banks and to Governor King at Port Jackson. It
is fair to say that King had unwittingly contributed to De
Caen's suspicions. He should not have asked Flinders to

carry a despatch to England, and he had omitted to give him the letter which Baudin had written asking that any English commander of a voyage of exploration should be given hospitality in a French port. Flinders cannot have known of the existence of the letter or he would have asked for it to be given to him. On learning that Flinders was being held prisoner, King wrote a letter to De Caen, but in it he referred to the way Baudin had been received in Port Jackson, which made matters worse, as De Caen disliked Baudin.

Flinders also wrote to William Marsden who was Secretary to the Admiralty, to Lord Wellesley (later Duke of Wellington, but at that time Governor General of India) and to Lord William Bentink, Governor of Madras which letter also concerned two residents of Mauritius, relatives of Pitot, who were imprisoned. They were released and Lord William himself wrote to De Caen. On learning that the French Admiral de Linois was in Mauritius, Flinders appealed to him, and immediately he wrote to Paris, but his approach to De Caen was useless, the two having such contempt for each other. Several requests were made to De Caen to allow Flinders to go to France, but although for a time his attitude appeared to soften, he sent a message counselling patience as he could do nothing until instructions were received from Paris.

Thomas Pitot sent several letters to France and in particular to the Comte de Bougainville, the French navigator, now a Conseiller d'Etat who succeeded in bringing the letter before Napoleon and his Council. Napoleon's interest in scientific discovery allowed him to take a generous view and he agreed that Flinders might be released, but the Ministry of Marine had other things to occupy them and it was sixteen months before a letter was received by De Caen in July 1807. It was intended to save everyone's face and whilst it approved of De Caen's action, it said that Flinders might be released: it was not an order to do so.

> Vous y verrez que votre conduite est approuvée et que, par un pur sentiment de générosité, le Gouvernement accorde au Capitaine Flinders sa liberté et la remise de son bâtiment.

The letter from Paris had been written when France and England were in "better intelligence than usual": now from a letter written by Colonel Montistrol it appeared that the Governor would release his prisoner, but that the time and manner of the release was left uncertain. Assuming that it would be fairly soon, Flinders asked to go to Port Louis to make arrangements but he was refused.

In August Flinders wrote again, suggesting the *Cumberland* should be sold, so that he could use part of the money to pay for his passage on a ship sailing as soon as possible, but he added that he would be prepared to risk taking the *Cumberland* if it was the only means by which he could leave the island. This would scarcely have been practical as the ship would now have deteriorated and the reply from the Governor's office said that she had been valued on arrival and that the money would be handed over on Flinders' departure but repeated that no arrangements had yet been made.

He answered that if he was to wait he would like the remainder of his books and papers returned, and after three weeks Colonel Monistrol invited him to come into Port Louis to collect them. On opening the trunk it was found that rats had played havoc with much of the paper, but fortunately the more important charts were intact, although thrown about. A request was made for the return of the journal which Flinders had been writing as he approached Mauritius and he was told that it was wanted for the purpose of making extracts, at which he expressed surprise as it had been in the Governor's possession for nearly four years. Colonel Monistrol then hinted that there was now doubt whether an application for release would be granted at the present time.

Whilst in town Flinders called on the owner of a ship used as a cartel, who had a house in Port Louis and who was prepared to offer a passage when his ship sailed. Some of the papers were put on board, because Flinders realized that he would be unlikely to be permitted to sail, but at least those papers could be taken to India and then forwarded home. Two other ships sailed, going to France, and a letter which Flinders wrote directly to the Minister of Marine in Paris was allowed to be sent.

In October Flinders wrote again to Colonel Monistrol saying that he would be relieved of much inquietude if he could be informed when it was the intention of His Excellency the Captain General to grant him the liberty which His Imperial and Royal Majesty had pleased to accord him, and why when ships were sailing for India and America he was not allowed to board them. He said he had suffered much and the uncertainty in which he had been kept was one of the bitterest ingredients in the cup and that it seemed he was to swallow the dregs to the last drop. He begged to know "at what period this waste of the best years of my life was to end".

The reply he received was as evasive as ever and Flinders began to wonder if he could break his parole which had been given to De Caen as the representative of the French Government, that Government having since given permission for him to leave. He debated it for some time before "deciding upon the line of conduct which duty

Flindersia australis, Botanical drawing
by Ferdinand Bauer 1802,
Natural History Museum, London.

Investigator off the Cumberland Isles
Oct. 10. 1802

My dearest love

Up to this day we are all well and the accomplishment of the objects of the voyage is advancing prosperously.

Amidst my various and constant occupations, thou art not one day forgotten. Be happy my beloved, rest assured of my faith and trust that I will return safely to soothe thy distresses, and repay thee for all thy anxieties concerning me.

Beg thy good father and mother to accept of my affectionate and respectful regards, as well as my friend Belle, and believe me to be thy own

Matt.w Flinders

I have not time to write to my father,—do thou for me.

Letter written by Matthew Flinders to his wife
from the Cumberland Islands 1802.
Flinders Collection: Flinders University, Adelaide.

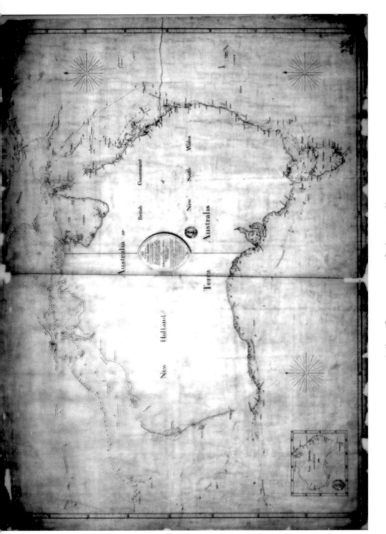

The first map of Australia.
Drawn by Matthew Flinders and sent to England in 1805.
United Kingdom Hydrographic Office.

A water colour by Ann Flinders, 1826:
an example of her flower paintings
Flinders Collection: Flinders University, Adelaide.

to my country, my family and myself prescribed to be right". He could not honourably break his parole, added to which he would have to leave behind all the work he had been doing.

Frustrated as he was over the next two and a half years his hatred for De Caen only increased and he began to believe that Decrès and De Caen had a private conspiracy not to release their prisoner because they thought he would go back to Australia to complete his work there, an honour they would prefer to have fallen to a Frenchman. Flinders' opinion was probably right, as others have since agreed.

Flinders was to know in 1808 that Péron in his "Voyage de Découvertes aux Terres Australes" was making claims that the French had been on the southern coast first and he had re-named various stretches calling them Terre Napoleon, Golfe Josephine and other French names. Kangaroo Island was transformed to Ile Decrès and the north coast of Van Diemen's Land discovered by Bass and Flinders in 1798 was claimed to be a discovery made by the French. Flinders was to learn that those who had sailed in Baudin's expedition were being honoured in France and it was being reported that Flinders' discoveries were only minimal. The fact that in his report Péron never mentioned Baudin's name, referring to him as the commander, throws light upon his character.

De Caen was taking the line that he had written to Paris explaining why Flinders was still held and was waiting for further instructions. Ships of the Royal Navy were frequently seen and it seemed likely that an invasion was planned — Napoleon himself expected it – because French ships were frequently harassing British merchant shipping in the Indian Ocean. De Caen had convinced himself that Flinders had come to Mauritius as a spy. Now he reasoned that because of his indulgence in allowing Flinders to meet residents of the island Flinders might have picked up information that he would pass on, in which case the wrath of Napoleon would have been vented on the Captain General. As it was, from the hill near Le Refuge, Flinders could see the red flag which indicated the sighting of British ships and he could often see the ships himself from the top of the hill. At one time, in desperation, he had formed a plan to signal to one of the ships, and then get the slave who acted as his servant to carry a trunk containing papers to a secluded bay at night, where a boat could land and take him on board.

Food was becoming scarce and Flinders joked that if only he was allowed to go home there would be one less mouth to feed. With invasion seeming imminent, De Caen was trying to get as many prisoners of war as possible off the island and there was one occasion when three Portuguese officers having been put on board a ship were unexpectedly returned to shore by the Captain. As the cartel sailed signals of recall were made, but too late. Flinders wrote "His Excellency was obliged to make use of a warm bath to prevent his anger from having an effect on his health".

In September 1809 Flinders was restricted to the immediate area around Le Refuge and not wishing to be sent to the Garden Prison he had to comply. Almost daily expecting to receive news about his release, he nevertheless continued his usual routine at Le Refuge, working out mathematical exercises and giving algebra and astronomy lessons in French to Madame D'Arifat's sons. A cartel was rumoured to be likely to leave for India shortly and a request was sent to Pitot to order some new clothes. He was rather slow about this, which seemed to indicate there was no immediate prospect of the cartel sailing but on

Wednesday 28th March 1810 the good news came at last. The entry in the diary reads:

> Fresh Ethy breeze, with occasional squalls of rain. Received a letter from colonel Monistrol, saying that the captain general authorised my return to my country in the cartel, upon condition of not serving hostilely against France and her allies during the course of the present war; this was accompanied with notes from M.M. Pitot and Hope felicitating me upon the event. Visited our neighbours Chevrean and Desfosses, preparatory to going to town. Mr and Mrs Lachenardier accompanied our family from the formers, here to supper, and I had the pleasure of beating Mr. Labauve at tric-trac. Sat up till one o'clock writing letters to my friends here.

11

Trim

By the time he left Mauritius, Flinders was running out of useful work he could do. In partnership with two others he had bought a piece of land on which they were raising cattle and he was reading widely in both the French and English languages, but in December 1809 he turned his hand to writing about the cat who had been such a wonderful friend during his years at sea and the first few months in prison.

The original manuscript, very neatly written with obvious care and love is owned by the Flinders family who have given permission for it to be reproduced in this book, and it is in the care of the National Maritime Museum, Greenwich. Flinders would be glad to know that Trim is now remembered by a small statue in a window of the State Library of New South Wales, Sydney and that he also has a memorial stone at the foot of his master's statue nearby.

For some reason Flinders changed the names of the ships: the *Investigator* becomes the *Spyall*, the *Reliance* the *Roundabout*, the *Porpoise* becomes the *Janty* and the *Cumberland* is named the *Minikin*.

To the memory of

TRIM

the best and most illustrious of his Race

the most affectionate of friends

faithful of servants

and best of creatures

He made a Tour of the Globe and a voyage to

Australia

which he circumnavigated and was ever the

delight and pleasure of his fellow voyagers

Returning to Europe in 1803 he was shipwrecked

in the Great Equinoxial Ocean

This danger escaped he sought refuge and assistance

at the Isle of France where

he was made prisoner contrary to the laws of

Justice of Humanity and of

French National Faith

and where alas! he terminated his useful

career by an untimely death

being devoured by the Catophagi of

that island

Many a time have I beheld his little merriments with
delight

and his superior intelligence with surprise

Never will his like be seen again

Trim was born in the Southern Indian Ocean in the

Year 1799 and

Perished as above at the Isle of France

in 1804

—

Peace be to his shade and

Honour to his memory

I can never speak of cats without a sentiment of regret for my poor Trim, the favourite of all our ship's company on the *Spyall*. This good-natured purring animal was born on board His Majesty's ship the *Roundabout* in 1799 during a passage from the Cape of Good Hope to Botany Bay; and saving the rights and titles of the Parish of Stepney, was consequently an Indian by birth. The signs of superior intelligence which marked his infancy procured for him an education beyond what is usually bestowed upon the individuals of his tribe; and being brought up amongst sailors, his manner acquired a peculiarity of cast which rendered them as different from those of other cats as the actions of a fearless seaman are from those of a lounging, shame-faced ploughboy. It was, however, from his gentleness and the innate goodness of his heart that I gave him the name of my uncle Toby's honest, kind-hearted, humble companion.

In playing with his little brothers and sisters upon deck by moonlight, when the ship was lying tranquilly in harbour, the energy and elasticity of his movements sometimes carried him so far beyond his mark that he fell overboard; but this was far from being a misfortune; he learned to swim and to have no dread of water; and when a rope was thrown over to him, he took hold of it like a man, and ran up it like a cat. In a short time he was able to mount up the gangway steps quicker than his master, or even than the first lieutenant.

Being a favourite with everybody on board, both officers and seamen, he was well fed, and grew fast both in size and comeliness. A description of his person will not be misplaced here. From the care that was taken of him, and the force of his own constitution, Trim grew to be one of the finest animals I ever saw. His size emulated that of his friends of Angora: his weight being from ten to twelve pounds, according as our *fresh-meatometer* stood high or low. His tail was long, large, and bushy; and when he was animated by the presence of a stranger of the anti-catean race, it bristled out to a fearful size, whilst vivid flashes darted from his fiery eyes, though at other times he was candour and good nature itself. His head was small and round — his physiognomy bespoke intelligence and confidence — his whiskers were long and graceful, and his ears were cropped in a beautiful curve. Trim's robe was a clear jet black, with the exception of his four feet, which seemed to have been dipped in snow, and his underlip, which rivalled them in whiteness. He had also a white star on his breast, and it seemed as if nature had designed him for the prince and model of his race: I doubt whether Whittington's cat, of which so much has been said and written, was to be compared to him.

Notwithstanding my great partiality to my friend Trim, strict justice obliges me to cite in this place a trait in his character which by many will be thought a blemish: he was, I am sorry to say it, excessively vain of his person, particularly of his snow-white feet. He would frequently place himself on the quarterdeck before the officers, in the middle of their walk; and spreading out his two white hands in the posture of the *lion couchant*, oblige them to stop and admire him. They would indeed say low to each other, "See the vanity of that cat!" but they could not help admiring his graceful form and beautiful white feet. Indeed, when it is known that to the finest form ever beheld he joined extraordinary personal and mental qualifications, the impossibility that the officers could be angry with him must be evident; and they were men of too much elevation of mind to be jealous of him. I would not be an advocate in the cause of vanity; but if it is ever excusable, it was so in this case. How many men are there, who have no claim either from birth, fortune, or acquirements, personal or mental, whose vanity is not to be confined within such harmless bounds, as was that of Trim! And I will say for him that he never spoke ill of or objected to the pretensions of others, which is more than can be said for very many bipeds.

Trim, though vain as we have seen, was not like those young men who, being assured of an independence, spend their youth in idle trifling, and consider all serious application as pedantic and derogatory, or at least to be useless; he was, on the contrary, animated with a noble zeal for the improvement of his faculties. His exercises commenced with acquiring the art of leaping over the hands; and as every man in the ship took pleasure in instructing him, he at length arrived to such a pitch of perfection that I am persuaded, had nature placed him in the empire of Lilliput, his merit would have promoted him to the first offices in the state.

He was taught to lie flat upon the deck on his back, with his four feet stretched out like one dead; and in this posture he would remain until a signal was given him to rise, whilst his preceptor resumed his walk backwards and forwards; if, however, he was kept in this position, which it must be confessed was not very agreeable to a quadruped, a slight motion of the end of his tail denoted the commencement of impatience, and his friends never pushed their lesson further.

Trim took a fancy to learning the art of nautical astronomy. When an officer took lunar or other observations, he would place himself by the timekeeper and consider the motion of the hands, and apparently the uses of the instrument, with much earnest attention. He would try to touch the second hand, listen to the ticking, and walk all round the piece to assure himself whether or no it might be a living animal; and mewing to the young gentleman whose business it was to mark down the time, seemed to ask an explanation. When the officer had made his observation, the cry of "Stop!" roused Trim from his meditations; he cocked his tail and, running up the rigging near to the officer, mewed at him to know the meaning of all those proceedings.

Finding at length that nature had not designed him for an astronomer, Trim had too much good sense to continue a useless pursuit; but a musket ball slung with a piece of twine, and made to whirl round upon the deck by a slight motion of the finger, never failed to attract his notice and to give him pleasure; perhaps from bearing a near resemblance to the movement of his favourite planet the moon, in her orbit round the primary which we inhabit. He was equally fond of making experiments upon projectile forces and the power of gravity. If a ball was thrown gently along the deck, he would pursue it; and when the gravitating principle combined with the friction overcame the impelling power, he would give the ball a fresh impetus, but generally to turn its direction into an elliptic curve (at other times the form of the earth appeared to be the object of his experiments, and his ball was made to describe an oblate spheroid). The seamen took advantage of his propensity to making experiments with globular bodies; and two of them would often place themselves, one at each end of the forecastle, and trundling a ball backwards and forwards from one to the other, would keep Trim in constant action running after it; his admiration of the planetary system having induced an habitual passion for everything round that was in motion. Could Trim have had the benefit of an Orrery, or of being present at Mr Walker's experiments in natural philosophy, there can be no doubt as to the progress he would have made in the sublimest of sciences.

His desire to gain a competent knowledge in practical seamanship was not less than he showed for experimental philosophy. The replacing of a topmast carried away, or taking a reef in the sails, were what most attracted his attention at sea; and at all times, when there was more bustle upon deck than usual, he never failed to be present and in the midst of it; for as I have before hinted, he was endowed with an unusual degree of confidence and courage, and having never received anything but good from men, he believed all to be his friends, and he was the friend of all. When the nature of the bustle upon deck was not understood by him, he would mew and rub his back up against the legs of one and the other, frequently at the risk of being trampled underfoot, until he obtained the attention of someone to satisfy him. He knew what good discipline required, and on taking in a reel, never presumed to go aloft until the order was issued; but so soon as the officer had given the words "Away up aloft!", up he jumped along with the seamen; and so active and zealous was he that none could reach the top before or so soon as he did. His zeal, however, never carried him beyond a sense of dignity: he did not lay out on the yard like a common seaman, but always remained seated upon the cap, to inspect like an officer. This assumption of authority to which, it must be confessed, his rank, though great as a quadruped, did not entitle him amongst men, created no jealousy; for he always found some good friend ready to caress him after the business was done, and to take him down in his arms.

In harbour, the measuring of log and lead lines upon deck, and the stowage of the holds below, were the favourite subjects of his attention. No sooner was a cask moved than he darted in under it upon the enemies of his king and country, at the imminent risk of having his head crushed to

atoms, which he several times very narrowly escaped. In the
bread room he was still more indefatigable; he frequently
solicited to be left there alone and in the dark, for two or
three days together, that nothing might interrupt him in the
discharge of his duty. This was one of the brightest traits
in my friend Trim's character, and would indeed do honour
to any character. In making the folio-wing deductions from
it I shall not, I think, be accused of an unjust partiality.
First, it must he evident that he had no fear of evil spirits,
and consequently that he had a conscience above reproach.
Second, it is clear that he possessed a degree of patience
and perseverance of which few men can boast; and third,
that like a faithful subject he employed all these estimable
qualities in the service of His Majesty's faithful servants,
and indirectly of His Majesty himself. Alas! my poor Trim,
thy extraordinary merit required only to be known, in order
to excite universal admiration.

Trim was admitted upon the table of almost every officer
and man in the ship: in the gunroom he was always the
first ready for dinner, but though he was commonly
seated a quarter of an hour before any other person, his
modest reserve was such that his voice was not heard until
everybody else was served. He then put in his request, not
for a full allowance — he was too modest — nor did he
desire there should be laid for him a plate, knife, fork or
spoon, with all which he could very well dispense, but by
a gentle caressing mew he petitioned for a little, little bit,
a kind of tythe from the plate of each; and it was to no
purpose to refuse it, for Trim was enterprising in time of
need, as he was gentle and well bred in ordinary times.
Without the greatest attention to each morsel, in the person
whom he had petitioned in vain, he would whip it off
the fork with his paw, on its passage to the mouth, with
such dexterity and an air so graceful that it rather excited

admiration than anger. He did not, however, leap off the table with his prize, as if he had done wrong; but putting the morsel into his mouth and eating it quietly, would go to the next person and repeat his little *mew*; if refused his wonted tythe, he stood ready to take all advantages. There are some men so inconsiderate as to be talking when they should be eating, who keep their meat suspended in mid-air till a semi-colon in the discourse gives an opportunity of taking their mouthful without interrupting their story. Guests of this description were a dead mark for Trim: when a short pause left them time to take the prepared mouthful, they were often surprised to find their meat gone, they could not tell how.

Trim had one day missed a fine morsel from the hungry activity of one of the young gentlemen who dined in the gunroom. Seeing him, however, talking and eating at the same time, my persevering gentleman did not give it up, though the piece was half masticated and only waited for a period to disappear; but running up the waistcoat of our unsuspecting guest, for Trim was then but a kitten, and placing one paw at each corner of his mouth, he laid vigorous siege to his morsel; and whilst the astonished midshipman inarticulately exclaimed, "G_d d_ _n the cat!" Trim fairly took the piece out of his mouth and carried it off. This was pushing his enterprises too far, and he therefore received a reprimand which prevented them in future.

The gunroom steward was, however, more particularly Trim's confidant; and though he had dined with the masters, he was not too proud to sit down a second time with the servant. William had such an opinion of Trim's intelligence that he talked to him as to his child, whilst my four-footed master, looking up in his face, seemed to understand him and to give rational answers. They had the following conversation after dinner on the day of Trim's audacious enterprise just related:

"Do you know, master Trim, that you have behaved very ill?" — Me-ew?

"It is very well to play your tricks with them that know you, but you should be more modest with strangers." — Mew!

"How dare you say that I gave you no breakfast? Did I not give you all the milk that was left, and some bread soaked in it?" — Mou-wow!

"No meat! What! you grow insolent? I'll chain you up; do you hear, Sir!" — Me-ew.

"Well, if you'll promise to behave better, you shall have a nice piece off the cold shank of mutton for your supper, you shall." — Mew-wew!

"Gently, master Trim. I'll give it you now, but first promise me upon your honour." — We-wee.

"Come then, my good boy, come up and kiss me."

Trim leaped up on his shoulder and, rubbing his face against William's cheek, received the mutton piece by piece out of his mouth.

In an expedition made to examine the northern parts of the coast of New South Wales, Trim presented a request to be of the party, promising to take upon himself the defence of our bread bags, and his services were accepted. Bongaree, an intelligent native of Port Jackson, was also on board our little sloop; and with him Trim formed an intimate acquaintance. If he had occasion to drink, he mewed to Bongaree and leaped up to the water cask; if to eat, he called him down below and went straight to his kid, where there was generally a remnant of black swan. In short, Bongaree was his great resource, and his kindness was repaid with caresses. In times of danger, Trim never showed any signs of fear; and it may truly be said that he never distrusted or was afraid of any man.

In 1800, the *Roundabout* returned to England by the way of Cape Horn and St Helena; and thus Trim, besides his other voyages, completed the tour of the globe. Many and curious are the observations which he made in various branches of science, particularly in the natural history of small quadrupeds, birds and flying fish, for which he had much taste. These, with his remarks upon man and manners, if future leisure should enable me to put into order, I may perhaps give to the world; and from the various seas and countries he has visited, joined to his superior powers for distinguishing obscure subjects, and talents for seizing them, these observations may be expected to be more interesting than the imaginary adventures of your guineas, shillings or half-pence, and to possess more originality than the Turkish spy.

Trim was not only a stranger to England, but also to a house and to the manner of living in it: the king of Bantam's ambassador was not more inexperienced in these matters than he. I took a lodging for him at Deptford, placing him under the guardianship of the good woman of the house, who promised to instruct him in the usages of terra firma; but she knew not what she had undertaken. He would go out at the sash window to the top of the house, for the convenience of making his observations on the surrounding country more at ease. If it came on to rain, the sash was put down. This would have been an invincible obstacle to other cats, but not so to Trim: he bolted through the glass like a clap of thunder, to the great alarm of the good hostess below. "Good Gad, Trim," exclaimed she on entering the chamber, "is it thee? They said thou wast a strange outlandish cat, and verily I think thou art the divil: I must shut thee up, for if thou go'st to treat neighbours thus, I shall have thee taken up for a burglary; but come, I know thy master will pay the damage: has thou cut thyself?"

Woe to the good woman's china if Trim got into her closet. Your delicate town-bred cats go mincing in amongst cups and saucers without touching them; but Trim! If he spied a mouse there he dashed at it like a man of war, through thick and thin: the splinters flew in all directions. The poor woman at first thought an evil spirit was playing pranks in her cupboard — she opens the door with fear and trembling when, to her infinite dismay, out jumps my black gentleman upon her shoulder: she was well nigh dead with fear. Seeing how much mischief was done to her dear china, the pride of her heart, she seized Trim to beat him soundly; but instead of trying to escape, the droll animal rubs his whiskers up against her chin and falls to purring. She had no longer the heart to strike him; but after a moment's hesitation, she heaved a sigh and picked up the pieces.

I took him up to London in the stage coach, and as there were no fine ladies to be frightened at the presence of a strange cat, he was left at full liberty. He was not in the least disconcerted by the novelty of his situation; but placing himself upon the seat, and stretching out his white paws, conducted himself reasonably like any other passenger; to the admiration of two gentlemen who did not cease to make inquiries concerning his education, manners, and adventures, during the whole way to town.

A worthy acquaintance in London took Trim into his family; but he soon requested me to take him back, for "such a strange animal," said he, "I never saw. I am afraid of losing him. He goes out into the streets in the middle of the day, and rubs himself against the legs of people passing by. Several have taken him up to caress him, but I fear someone will be carrying him off."

I took him on board the *Spyall* to make a second voyage to the South Seas. Trim now found himself at home; and his gentleness and extraordinary confidence, joined to the amusement his droll antics furnished them, soon made him as great a favourite with his new shipmates as he had been on board the *Roundabout*.

We had several dogs on board the *Spyall*, but Trim was undisputed master of them all. When they were at play upon the deck, he would go in amongst them with his stately air; and giving a blow at the eyes of one, and a scratch on the nose to another, oblige them to stand out of his way. He was capable of being animated against a dog, as dogs usually may be against a cat; and I have more than once sent him from the quarter-deck to drive a dog off the forecastle. He would run half the way briskly, crouching like a lion which has prey in view; but then, assuming a majestic deportment, and without being deterred by the menacing attitude of his opponent, he would march straight up to him and give him a blow on the nose, accompanied with a threatening *mew*! If the dog did not immediately retreat, Trim flew at him with his war cry of *Yow*! If resistance was still made, he leaped up on the rail over his head and so bespattered him about the eyes that he was glad to run off howling. Trim pursued him till he took refuge below; and then returned smiling to his master to receive his caresses.

During our circumnavigation of Australia in the years 1801, 1802 and 1803, Trim had frequent opportunities of repeating his observations and experiments in his favourite

science, natural history, and of exerting his undiminished
activity and zeal for the public good. In the Gulf of
Carpentaria, from the unhealthiness of the climate, the
want of his usual fresh food, and perhaps from too much
application to study, this worthy creature became almost
grey, lost much of weight, and seemed to be threatened
with a premature old age; but to the great joy of his friends,
he re-assumed his fine black robe and his accustomed
portliness, a short time after returning to harbour.

Only once was Trim known to be guilty of theft: he had
a soul above it; but one unlucky afternoon a cold leg of
mutton in the pantry tempted him. Being unable to carry
it off himself, he got the assistance of Van, a Dutch cat
on board; and they had so far succeeded as to get it down
off the shelf, and were dragging it together into the hold,
when lo! the steward came and surprised them in the act.
Van made his escape, but Trim, ever confident, made no
efforts, and was seized and beaten soundly. He took the
blows with philosophical patience; but no sooner was he
set at liberty than he ran after his false Dutch friend, and
repaid him with interest the beating he had received. The
recital of this unfortunate anecdote of my friend Trim
will, I hope, be received as a proof of the impartiality of
the history; and I advertise the reader not to seek in it for
any political allegory, but to be assured that the facts were
really such as they are here related.

The *Spyall* being found to be rotten, Trim embarked on
board His Majesty's ship the *Janty* to return to England,
and was shipwrecked with us upon a coral bank in the
Great Equinoxial Ocean on the night of August 17, 1803.
The imagination can scarcely attain to what Trim had to
suffer during this dreadful night, but his courage was not
beaten down. He got to Wreck Reef Bank with the crew,
and passed there two long and dreary months, during

which his zeal in the provision tent was not less than it had been in the bread room, and his manners preserved all their amiability. When vessels arrived to our assistance, Trim preferred following his master on board the *Minikin* schooner to going with the rest of the ship's company to China in a large vessel, giving thereby a memorable example of faithful attachment.

The *Minikin*, being very leaky, was obliged to stop at the Isle of France; and there poor Trim, his master and few followers were all made prisoners, under the pretext that they had come to spy out the nakedness of the land, though it was clear as day that they knew nothing of the war that had taken place a few months before. Trim was confined in a room with his master and another officer; and as he possessed more philosophy than we did, he contributed by his gay humour to soften our straight captivity; but sometimes also he contrived to elude the vigilance of the sentinel at the door, and left us to make little temporary excursions in the neighbourhood. It is probable that he made some new secret acquaintances in these visits, for they became more frequent than was prudent; and for fear of accidents, we were obliged to shut him up after supper.

On our being removed to the Maison Despeaux amongst the prisoners of war, a French lady offered to be Trim's security, in order to have him for a companion to her little daughter; and the fear of some clandestine proceedings on the part of the soldiers of the guard induced me to comply, on finding it would give no umbrage to His Excellency the French governor and captain-general. A fortnight had scarcely passed when the public gazette of the island announced that Trim was nowhere to be found, and offered a reward of ten Spanish dollars to anyone who would conduct him back to his afflicted little mistress. My sorrow may be better conceived than described; I would with pleasure have given fifty dollars to have had my friend and companion restored to me. All research and offers of recompense were in vain, poor Trim was effectually lost; and it is but too probable that this excellent unsuspecting animal was stewed and eaten by some hungry black slave, in whose eyes all his merits could not balance against the avidity excited by his sleek body and fine furred skin.

Thus perished my faithful intelligent Trim! The sporting, affectionate and useful companion of my voyages during four years. Never, my Trim, "to take thee all in all, shall I see thy like again"; but never wilt thou cease to be regretted by all who had the pleasure of knowing thee. And for thy affectionate master and friend, he promises thee, if ever he shall have the happiness to enjoy repose in his native country, under a thatched cottage surrounded by half an acre of land, to erect in the most retired corner a monument to perpetuate thy memory and record thy uncommon merits.

12

Freedom

As his instructions were that he should sail in the *Harriet* which was waiting in the harbour Flinders said his farewells to Madame D'Arifat and went down to Port Louis the following day. The next morning he was invited to breakfast by the commander of the cartel, Captain Ramsden and Mr. Hope, the commissioner of the prisoners who were being exchanged, and at dinner that evening he met a number of his fellow passengers after which a party was held which went on until after midnight. A call was made on Colonel Monistrol to ask yet again for the return of the journal which had been confiscated and to enquire about the fate of the *Cumberland*, and Flinders was promised that the Governor would be asked about this, but nothing came of it.

During the next few days many people, some of whom he did not know, paid calls to wish him well and he was allowed to spend one night at the country home of the Pitots. A great cavalcade set out, singing songs composed by Thomi Pitot in one of which was a special verse praising the English and hoping that the two nations might soon be as united as the present gathering of French and English. Dancing continued until daylight, stopping only for supper at two o'clock in the morning. A week later there was another large gathering and a toast was drunk to Ann, to which Flinders replied in fluent French, which met with acclamation.

The social round continued, but there was still no fixed date for the *Harriet* to sail. At last on the 9th May, forty days after he had left Le Refuge, Flinders was told to board the ship. The Pitots bade him farewell and to mark the occasion he was given a diploma as a corresponding member of the Societé d'Emulation.

There was to be still further delay, the reason being that British ships were frequently in sight and a convoy of ships bringing urgently needed supplies from France was expected, as was widely known in Port Louis. Although the *Harriet* was supposed to sail for Bengal without making direct contact with a British ship, it was feared she might do so and that some of the prisoners of war might give away information which would lead to the interception of the convoy. Orders were given that no-one was to go ashore and the time had to be passed in playing cards and reading. Flinders thought that he might one day return to finish his explorations and he started to teach himself the Malay language which would be useful if he ever called in at Kupang or encountered the Malay prows again.

Finally, after eleven weeks in Port Louis, Flinders received back his sword, but not his two spy glasses or the journal. He had to sign a further parole promising on his word of honour not to act in any service which might be considered as directly or indirectly hostile to France. It was also said that he might leave by way of Bengal, but did not stipulate that he must do so. The officer delivering the parole remarked that he supposed Flinders would not waste time and would go to the Cape of Good Hope in the first vessel encountered.

On 27th June the pilot came on board, the anchor was weighed, but in swinging out the ship touched a sandbank and stuck fast for about three hours. The French ship

L'Estaffe was seen carrying a flag of truce, coming from the British squadron, which caused concern in case she was bringing a message which might annoy the Governor and cause him to cancel the sailing of the *Harriet*, but luckily they got off the bank before *L'Estaffe* reached the harbour.

Out in the open sea after his long captivity Flinders "had the inexpressible pleasure of being out of reach of General De Caen."

Three frigates and a sloop of war composed the British squadron they could see, but instead of coming towards them, they stood away and it was supposed that the Commodore had given an undertaking not to communicate with the cartel. Flinders did not wish to lose the chance of making contact, and he persuaded Ramsden, the commander, to follow the ships. Ramsden got near enough to go towards them in a boat when a letter left by *L'Estaffe* was handed over the side, and it was as they had supposed. Flinders asked to be taken on board as having studied the letter it was agreed that this would not break any rules and in any case the *Harriet* had not received a copy having got out of Port Louis before *L'Estaffe* had come into the harbour. By great good fortune the sloop of war, the *Otter* was to leave for the Cape of Good Hope the following day, so having been asked to dine with the Commodore, Flinders transferred to the *Otter* but was soon to discover that one of his trunks had been left aboard the *Harriet*. It did finally reach him in London, but not until October 1811. By 11th July Simon's Town was reached, where a signal was received indicating that the Commanding Officer wished to see Flinders immediately. As he rode over to see him he had the mortification to see a ship destined for England sailing out of the bay and was told that he would probably have to wait six weeks for another ship. When calling on the Admiral he was asked to show the parole he had signed, which stated that he must not take part in active service, but the Admiral decided that he was not under an obligation to refuse information about Mauritius and requested immediate written answers to a number of questions.

In his talks with the Admiral Flinders probably became aware of the part played by Hugh Hope, the commissioner for prisoners in Mauritius. Whilst he had been thinking despairingly that he had been forgotten it is possible that for some time the British Government had guessed that De Caen was using Flinders as a pawn so that in the likely event of an invasion of the island which he knew all too well he could not defend, he would have means to negotiate. It is thought that Hope may have been given authority by Lord Minto, Governor General of India to discuss terms with De Caen in strict secrecy and if he would release his prisoner, then when British troops landed he would surrender, but he would not be kept a prisoner of war, nor would any member of his garrison.

The naval blockade of the island continued and it was not until 29th November that a British force landed. De Caen put up a show of resistance, but by 3rd December he had agreed to surrender and within three weeks he had left for France. De Caen did ask that the local population should not be penalised and this was agreed as the British had already stated that their laws, liberties and customs would be respected and in August had managed to circulate leaflets to this effect. In view of the gratitude which Flinders felt towards the people of Mauritius, it is something which he must have supported whole heartedly.

Again time was wasted. There was little work he could do, but he bathed in the cascade below Table Mountain, made a few brief visits in the neighbourhood and joined in the social life, commenting that the Dutch women were not so elegant as the French. He was not allowed to keep a diary whilst a passenger aboard the *Otter*, but he kept one whilst at the Cape and like his diary in Mauritius it gives us a record of life there at the time.

At the end of August he left the Cape as a passenger in H.M.S. *Olympia* and in two weeks reached St. Helena, where they stayed only for a few hours to take on water, passed the Azores and entered the English Channel on the 20th October. A strong gale got up near the dangerous Casket Rocks: they were blown towards the French coast and it was not until the wind had moderated on the 23rd that they sighted Portland Bill, anchoring for the night at Studland Bay before continuing to Spithead. It had been a run of six weeks from St Helena "which in an indifferent vessel, very leaky and excessively ill-found, must be considered an excellent passage".

The story is told that when James Cook in his battered ship the *Endeavour* passed Spithead on his way up the Channel, the King's ships there fired a salute of welcome. No such welcome awaited Flinders when the *Olympia* dropped anchor on 24th October 1810, but thankful to be home he slipped quietly ashore and took the coach to London that evening, having been away for nine years and three months, held six and a half years a captive, and not having heard from his wife or any member of his family for four and a half years.

On his arrival in London at 7.30 in the morning, Flinders took rooms at the Norfolk Hotel in the Strand. His first call was at the Admiralty where he was greeted warmly by both the First and Second Secretaries. Immediately afterwards he got in touch with his agent who had acted for him during the years he was away and who would know the whereabouts of Ann. She had received a letter written by Sir Joseph Banks on 25th September saying that it gave him infinite pleasure to tell her that he had heard from the Admiralty that her husband was expected home within a few weeks. Ann then came to London to stay with Mrs. Penelope Proctor, a relative of Flinders.

The news soon got round and John Franklin came to call during the morning and whilst they were sitting talking there was a knock on the door and Ann was shown in. The diary simply records "At noon my Mrs F came to me." Both had changed. Aged thirty six, Flinders' dark hair was almost white and the youthful colouring of his face was gone: the years of anxiety which, after the initial shock and deep hurt and unhappiness, Ann had borne with courage and composure had left their mark, but their love remained. John Franklin left the room hastily and wrote later to apologise, saying he "felt so sensibly the affecting scene of your meeting with Mrs. Flinders that I would not have remained any longer in the room under any consideration".

A summons arrived from the First Lord of the Admiralty, who also welcomed him warmly. Ann had to wait with Mrs. Proctor, but when Flinders came back with the news that he had been promoted to Post Captain, they all dined together.

The following morning the diary records that Flinders had his hair cut and went to a tailor to be measured for new clothes — an important matter with the winter months approaching. Although visitors called and there were many matters to attend to, they had ten days together to pick up the threads of their marriage. Ann had received letters from Mauritius, but he had been without news of her, possibly because even through Flinder's London agent it was difficult to find anyone who could carry a letter or see it on its complicated journey. Her husband however occasionally did have the chance to entrust letters to prisoners of war who were released, or to Thomi Pitot who had contact with trading ships such as those who came to Mauritius from America to buy coffee. After the fall of Mauritius to the British in December 1810 it became apparent that a number of letters had simply not been delivered as they were found in an office in Port Louis. A letter Ann wrote in 1808 arrived back in London with a packet of other letters in March 1811 and a further bundle of letters forwarded from Port Jackson to Mauritius was found in June of the same year.

On the 5th November a move was made to rooms in King Street, not far from Sir Joseph Banks' London home in Soho Square. Although they were furnished it was quite customary to rent rooms in this way and Ann must have felt that at last she had a home of her own.

One of the first things that had to be done was to write to Sir Joseph who was still at Revesby Abbey in Lincolnshire and preliminary discussions started with the officials at the Admiralty concerning the formal writing of the history of the voyage of the *Investigator*. Flinders also raised the question of his promotion, which had been dated from 7th May 1810, the day of his release in Mauritius. The Admiralty maintained that it could not be made earlier, although they conceded that if he had returned home safely in 1803 he would have received promotion then, as had been promised by Earl Spencer before the *Investigator* sailed. It was argued that at least promotion should have been dated from the time when the French Government had agreed to his liberation, after which De Caen did not have official authority to detain him. The Admiralty, always looking for economies and terrified of creating a precedent, would not agree, and would not take account of the fact that when in Mauritius Flinders had worked assiduously on his reports and charts, some of which he had been able to send home.

When Banks returned to London on 7th November he invited Flinders to call to discuss the writing of the account of the voyage, and a brief mention was made about the date of promotion. Banks was sympathetic and advised Flinders to write a Memorial to the Admiralty, which he did at once.

On the same day he was invited to dine with the members of the board of the East India Company who told him they would honour their promise to pay £600 towards the costs of the provisions for the officers and scientists aboard the *Investigator*. The commander was to receive £300 and the rest was to be divided amongst the others. When the money was paid over they met for a celebratory dinner: Aken, now the captain of a merchant ship, was at sea, but later Flinders and Aken met for dinner, together with their wives. Hugh Bell, the surgeon had died, but his heir was traced and a small sum was also given to Robert Purdie who had acted as his mate.

Another immediate care was to take up the cases of the French prisoners of war held in England and in particular those who came from Mauritius. Early in November he journeyed down to Odiham in Hampshire to visit them and take them letters from their relatives, as well as making financial arrangement for one of them who had been captured recently. His efforts meant that within a short time five of them were sent back to Mauritius. He was to continue to take up cases of other prisoners, not all of whom he could help, but he always replied to their letters.

At last Flinders was to learn the fate of the *Investigator*. In May 1804 work had been started to strip down the hulk that was still in the harbour at Sydney Cove. One of her decks was removed, so she must have looked much as she had done when the Admiralty first bought her as a coastal vessel. A run was made to Norfolk Island before Governor King decided to send the ship to England carrying despatches. Before leaving, another plant house was placed on the deck for the live plants and Robert Brown and Ferdinand Bauer travelling as passengers took with them in their cabins the collection of seeds and dried plants carefully wrapped in paper. They sailed at the end of May 1805.

Her new commander was none other than William Kent who had so skilfully brought back the *Supply* from South Africa to Port Jackson in 1797. On this occasion he had his wife and three young children with him. The passage back to England had been equally hazardous: rounding Cape Horn the deck was almost continually awash. After crossing the Atlantic, Kent did not dare take the ship into the English Channel in case the autumn gales blew her towards the French coast, but went round the north of Ireland and arrived at Liverpool on 12th October 1805. Brown and Kent recorded that the crazy, cut down *Investigator* was perhaps the most deplorable ship in the world: she arrived covered in barnacles and her sails showing the signs of an abandoned vessel.

The plant house had to be taken off and the dried plants and the drawings had to be re-wrapped because of the excessive damp in the cabins. Brown then insisted that the collection must be taken to London by road, where he and Bauer did not have much of a welcome. The Admiralty had other things to consider — news of the Battle of Trafalgar had just been received.

Kent was ordered to proceed to Plymouth but unable to go further he put in at Falmouth. After patching up, the ship was used for coastal duties for four years before being broken up in Pembroke Dock.

* * *

By Friday 23rd November, all was ready for the long promised holiday. Unfortunately they missed by five minutes the coach which was to take them to Cambridge and they had to travel by post chaise to catch up with it. The following day they continued to Wisbech, staying with relatives and continuing on Sunday afternoon to Tydd St. Mary, the home of Charles Hursthouse, who was Executor of the Will of Flinders' father, because arrangements had to be made for the transfer of a legacy of £600 with the accrued interest. Samuel had already received a similar legacy. After two days at Tydd Charles Hursthouse drove them in his curricle to Spalding. They met Flinders' uncle John and dined at the White Hart before continuing to Donington for a week's stay. However the family he had left when he last saw them in 1801 was sadly depleted. Elizabeth, his sister, had married unhappily and had since died, leaving two children. There had always been trouble with John, his brother, who had a violent temperament and had been sent to a school in Spalding for two years to get him away from some of the rough company he kept in Donington. He had become worse and by the end of 1802 his father had written that "my very unfortunate Son John is returned upon my hands and in a state terrible to conceive": it was impossible for him to find employment and "we are leaving no stone unturned to find a proper receptable for him". He had been sent to live at York Lunatic Asylum and a financial provision had to be made for him. The third sadness was the death of John Franklin's mother, who was Mrs Flinders' sister, and from whose funeral she had just returned.

During the visit relatives and friends called or came to dine and Flinders' other sister, Susanna, now married to George Pearson, came over from Boston to spend a night. Flinders helped his step-mother with a number of problems arising from his father's Will and very carefully went through the accounts for her. He began to take an interest in the history of his family, visited the church and appears to have made a decision to put up some memorial tablets.

By 4th December it was time to leave, and without thinking that he would never see Donington again, they went happily to Boston to stay with the Pearsons. More relatives and friends called, including John Allen, the miner aboard the *Investigator*. George Pearson was a Baptist and Susanna's marriage to him had not met with the approval of her father. However, Ann and Matthew were more broad minded and they accompanied them to listen to a preacher at the Baptist Church in Boston's High Street. As a belated wedding present to his sister, a handsome copper tea urn was bought, to which was attached an engraved silver plate, and it is still in the possession of one of Susanna's descendants. The diary tells us that sweetmeats were also bought for the children.

Having spent four days in Boston they set off in a post chaise for the Franklin's home at Mavis Enderby. The following morning Flinders and his cousin Willingham walked three miles through the snow to Spilsby, where visits were paid to several people and where a payment of £200 due to him from the Will of his mother's brother was settled.

Like her father, Ann suffered from very severe headaches

and unfortunately was stricken with one when staying with the Franklins, but she recovered in twenty-four hours and was well enough to visit Partney to stay a night there. Her step-father had died in 1808, their home had been sold and Mrs Tyler had moved about making long visits to friends before she had bought a house at Beverley. In the diary it is recorded that they went about Partney to visit Ann's old friends, nurses and servants "to all of which she wished to show her lion and give some trifle".

The last part of their holiday was spent with Ann's relations at Hull and they must have visited her mother, but unfortunately twelve pages are missing from the diary. On 2nd January 1811 it is recorded they started their journey back from Barton on Humber to London, travelling thirty-four hours by coach with only stops for meals.

Perhaps not surprisingly two days later Ann suffered from one of her headaches and had to stay in bed.

13

The Years in London

From that time on, January 1811, Flinders worked steadily, first considering how he was to get the detailed account of his voyage written and the charts engraved. His first call was on Sir Joseph Banks, when it was agreed that a meeting should take place at the Admiralty to discuss whether an author should be engaged to help with the official account, as Flinders had doubted he could write it alone. Years before he had written to Willingham Franklin asking if he might be interested to help, but saying that a knowledge of mathematics would be needed. It was now decided that Flinders himself should write the account, but that a committee should be formed consisting of Joseph Banks, Charles Philip Yorke, the First Lord of the Admiralty, and John Barrow, the second Secretary to the Admiralty,

The costs of the production had to be discussed. Flinders had been put on half pay amounting to £300 a year because he was not on active service — indeed he could not be, because of the terms of the parole. In spite of the war there was communication between Paris and London and he was released from that parole a year later. He pointed out that he could not take other employment as his time would be fully taken up, and furthermore he would have to live in London which would be much more expensive than living in the country.

Whilst the Admiralty would pay for the costs of reducing and engraving the charts, Flinders was to meet the costs of paper, printing and the fees of the two artists, but he would be allowed to keep the profits of the book when it was published. He estimated that his expenses would be between £500 and £600, so that it was clear that while he completed the work for which he had been commissioned in 1801 he was going to suffer financial hardship. The Admiralty was adamant that he remain on half pay. However, later on and through the influence of Banks a loan was made of £200, which Banks said was not expected to be re-paid. It was a curious way to hide expenditure in the Admiralty's accounts.

The question of back dating the time of his promotion was raised again, but now Banks advised him to forget it. He felt he could not do this as apart from the financial loss, if he was to stay in the Navy and aspire to flag rank, the loss of seniority would tell against him.

In 1801 Earl Spencer, then First Lord of the Admiralty had told Flinders that he would be promoted to Post Captain on the completion of his tour which was expected to be the end of 1803. It was only the rotten state of the ship with which he had been provided that had forced him to omit the serious charting of the western coast. Furthermore although prisoners of war did not receive promotion during the time they were held, Flinders had been classified by the French as a prisoner of the state and thus had been able to do a considerable amount of work during the years of his detention, some of which, including the first map of the outline of Australia, had been sent home.

The First Secretary to the Admiralty, John Croker, indicated that the memorandum Flinders had written would not be submitted to the King in Council. George III had always been interested in discoveries and he would have known from Banks about the sailing of the *Investigator* in 1801. Had he not now been lapsing into his last, sad, illness, the outcome might have been different. As it was the Prince of Wales was appointed Regent. Flinders happened to meet his librarian who tried to arrange an audience, but the Prince Regent was not interested.

Yorke seemed to be avoiding Flinders and Banks had given up his attempts to ask for reconsideration, but a final attempt was made by William Wilberforce (best known for his work to abolish the slave trade). It was the resourceful Henrietta Flinders, who had been governess to the children of Admiral Pasley, who wrote to him initially; she was now married and living in Hull for which Wilberforce was the Member of Parliament. Wilberforce discussed it with the First Lord of the Admiralty, and not convinced by the explanation he received, he offered to raise it on the floor of the House of Commons. After seeking advice from others, Flinders decided that this might jeopardise the publication of his work and that it would be unwise to get involved in political controversy, a view with which Wilberforce then agreed.

Later, when Flinders in company with William Bligh, who was now an Admiral, was invited to meet the Duke of Clarence — the future William IV — to discuss the voyage of the *Investigator* and to show his charts, it seemed that the Duke was willing to intervene. However, the Admiralty, still terrified that a precedent would be created, refused to consider the matter further. Coupled with the fact of being put on half pay and certainly suffering financial hardship, Flinders increasingly felt that he was treated shabbily and those in high places showed a lack of understanding of what he had achieved.

Nevertheless, the work began. The charts were assembled

and decisions made as to which ones Arrowsmith, the official printer, should reduce and engrave. William Westall was sent for and decisions made about which of his sketches should accompany the charts, a total of twenty eight being selected initially. Ferdinand Bauer was consulted about his botanical drawings and Robert Brown, now secretary to Banks, was brought into the discussions.

William Bligh, lately returned from his somewhat unsuccessful governorship of New South Wales, joined in and was surprisingly helpful, while it soon appeared that Joseph Banks did not understand the great extent of the Australian coastline or the work that had already gone in to making the charts. The lunar charts for the years 1801, 1802 and 1803 supplied to the *Investigator* by the Board of Longitude were found to contain inaccuracies, and therefore it was decided that John Crosley and Samuel Flinders should be entrusted with the extremely lengthy and complex task of checking all the measurements.

From the time Samuel had returned to England in 1804 he had served in a number of ships and had been given command of the *Bloodhound*, a 12-gun brig. In 1808 he had been brought to court charged with disobedience to orders and making incorrect entries in the log book. Although the charges were untrue, Samuel defended himself in a way which upset the court and he was discharged from the ship. His seniority was degraded by three years and he was put on half pay which angered him to the extent that he did not bother to keep his name on the Navy List. His older brother felt he had to try to help him and wrote to his squadron commander to describe Samuel's work on the voyage round Australia. Samuel's name was restored to the Navy List, and an agreement made to pay him £250 for the work which now had to be done. Although

Samuel was temperamental, he had worked on the books recording the observations and measurements taken aboard the *Investigator* and so he was the best person to undertake these corrections under the supervision of the astronomer, John Crosley.

On the 20th January Flinders took the stage coach to Greenwich as he had been invited to dine with Sir Nevil Maskelyne, the now ageing Astronomer Royal, with whom he hoped to have a useful discussion about the observations made in the *Investigator*, but it was not a successful meeting as Sir Nevil appeared unwell, and in fact he died three weeks later.

Meetings followed meetings and decisions had to be made about the costs of reducing and engraving the charts. Westall produced the coastal sketches which he had made for use in conjunction with the charts, so that coastal features could be recognised. Banks asked for Aaron Arrowsmith to come to Soho Square with Flinders so that he could completely understand them before he took them to the Admiralty to get approval for an order to be given. As is still the way today, when matters have to be settled by committees, the bureaucratic wheels moved slowly, and it took time to reach decisions.

Although there were frequent callers at King Street and although her husband was out a great deal, Ann must have rejoiced in having him at home when he was writing and appreciated the quiet times they had together. However, in March there was an upset, and the entry in the diary says that they had stupidly accepted an invitation from their landlady to join her and some of her friends for dinner. What actually happened is not recorded, but the other guests are described as goths, and the next day a hasty removal was made to Nassau Street, not far away.

In April Henrietta, Flinders' half sister, arrived to stay and Ann's half sister, Belle, joined them soon afterwards. Because of lack of space this did make it difficult for work to be done at the writing table, but nevertheless the girls were entertained. A piano was hired for Henrietta, and perhaps the flute which had been played so often in Mauritius was used to accompany her. There were outings to Kew Gardens to see the plants grown from seeds collected on the *Investigator's* voyage, they went to see Westall's collection of pictures, they visited St Paul's and spent an evening at Vauxhall Gardens from which they did not return until 2.00 in the morning. Days were spent with Ann's relations, the Hippins family who lived at Hackney, which was still outside London. On one visit they joined a large crowd to watch the taking off of a balloon carrying two men. Samuel often joined them and escorted the girls for walks. It was thought that Samuel might make a suitable husband for Belle, but she was quite decisive that she would not have him.

By the time they left in July Flinders was becoming increasingly hard worked and concerned about the immense task he was undertaking. He had set aside much of the work on the charts whilst he waited for the recalculations of the lunar tables and he had turned to writing the lengthy introduction to the book. This sets out accounts of the navigators known to have sighted the coasts of Australia as well as his own exploits and those of George Bass whilst serving in the *Reliance*. It runs to 204 pages and was completed by December 1811. Still showing his passion for discovery he asks at the end why it should be thought necessary to send another expedition (by which he meant his own voyage in the *Investigator*) and answers that there was ample room for two or three ships to be employed for years with a zeal and perseverance not inferior to the examples given by the best navigators.

At the same time he had to attend to the financial affairs of his family and to write letters in answer to requests from young men seeking to join the Navy. He wrote up his journal each day and still corresponded with Madame D'Arifat, Thomi Pitot and Charles Desbassayn, the latter about the property he had bought for Flinders in the Isle of Bourbon, and he learnt of the marriage of Delphine. Now that Mauritius and Bourbon were in British hands letters came through, although because of the distance they took about five months to arrive.

Like his father he kept a strict eye on his investments and did not want to draw on them for living expenses, but his meagre pay meant that those expenses were a constant cause for concern. In a letter to Madame D'Arifat he told her how happy he was, except for the fact that he had financial worries because of having to live on half pay.

A new Astronomer Royal, John Pond, had been appointed, but the Board of Longitude were continuing to vacillate about a decision to appoint John Crosley and Samuel Flinders to recalculate the astronomical observations. The work was essential to the final accuracy of the charts. On 16th July it was announced that John Crosley should do the work and not surprisingly Samuel Flinders was extremely angry as he had been working on the recalculations since April. He wrote several intemperate letters to the Board and in a letter to the Astronomer Royal said that not only would he cease work, but that he would retain both his own and his brother's record books. In an attempt to smooth it over Matthew asked him to hand back those books which he himself had compiled: without them the recalculations could not be made. Samuel refused. This resulted in an unpleasant quarrel, the elder brother having to write a firm letter saying that if the books were not handed over, then all communication between them must cease. It was explained that not only was Samuel laying himself open to prosecution by the Board of Longitude, who legally owned the books, but that he was being very hurtful to Matthew. Samuel gave in, but said he was only doing it as a favour to his brother. In the end the Board of Longitude agreed to the original arrangement and Samuel received £50 in advance and £200 on completion of the work, but much time had been wasted.

By the autumn it was decided that a move should be made to a house not far from the road leading to Hampstead and from which there was a pleasant view across the fields. Ann seems to have suffered more headaches than usual when living in Nassau Street, and it was thought that opportunities to take walks in the fresher air might help her. Another consideration was that she was pregnant and if they lived further out of the town they might perhaps expect fewer casual callers — something that Flinders would also welcome so that his writing was not interrupted so frequently. Later they were to go back to the Soho area, presumably because it proved inconvenient to be at a distance from Banks' house and the Admiralty, and even then they were to move three more times.

Ann was well during the rest of her pregnancy, and the coming baby was nicknamed Timothy. Nevertheless she was fearful: it was all too common for women to die in childbirth, and she was forty which added to the risk. She wrote a long and sad letter to Matthew which she asked to be given to him if she died. If the child survived Ann asked him to care for it and she repeatedly expressed her love and thanked him for his love for her, adding that if God would be pleased to spare her life it would enable her to show her love for many years to come. It is surprising that when Ann destroyed her other letters to Matthew she kept this one. It is a very personal, dignified letter expressing her deep love: although it has been published, it is questionable whether she would have wished others to read it even two hundred years later.

Belle Tyler came to stay again to take charge of the household and on the morning of 1st April, Matthew called her asking her to go to her sister. Her reply was "Nonsense, you will not make an April Fool of me" — but the baby was born that afternoon. In keeping with the tradition of her maternal grandmother's family, she was named Anne, the spelling being changed with each generation. The following day Matthew wrote to his step-mother showing the obvious delight he had in the safe arrival of his daughter.

Ann recovered quickly, but a few days later Matthew was very unwell with another attack of his "gravelly complaint", but he continued with his work and recovered within a few days. On 19th April he travelled to Chatham where arrangements were being made for testing Flinders' work on the effects of magnetism. These arrangements were far from satisfactory and together with the squalls of winds coming from the north, it was difficult to make as conclusive a report as had been hoped. However, Thomas Hurd, the Chief Hydrographer at the Admiralty asked that further experiments should be made at Portsmouth in May and those were considered successful.

Joseph Banks suggested that the writing of the book should be set aside for a time whilst Flinders concentrated on the report of these experiments. The Admiralty agreed and over the next month a forty-five page document was produced.

When it was taken to the Hydrographer at the Admiralty

it lay on his desk for about two weeks, when on making an enquiry, Flinders was told that it would have to be referred to the Astronomer Royal or the Board of Longitude. He realised that no-one at the Admiralty was sufficiently competent to give an opinion, and his discovery ran the risk of being put aside. However, Sir Joseph Banks intervened and tactfully suggested that the Admiralty should consult him. Thus, in the time honoured way, no-one at the Admiralty would be taking responsibility, but they could not be accused of neglecting it. By the end of August Flinders was asked to reduce his report and this was eventually circulated to the commanders of all the Navy's ships. Perhaps typically with anything new, not all of them would be impressed by the recommendation that an iron bar be placed near the compass to correct errors.

As he had done in Mauritius, Flinders recorded social events during his years in London. He often dined out, with his wife accompanying him occasionally and frequently visitors dined with them, including two of John Franklin's sisters, Sarah and Isabella, and other Lincolnshire relatives who were visiting London. Visits were exchanged with Flinders' cousins, the Proctors, with Ann's relations, the Hippins family, and Samuel was often a guest. Two members of the Desbassayn family from Mauritius were staying in England, and visits were exchanged. When he was in London Joseph Banks invited Flinders to his Sunday evenings of conversation where guests were scholars and academics of distinction, and there were two occasions when Lady Banks invited them both to dinner.

Flinders continued to correspond with Thomas Pitot to help make representations to the British Government for payments to cover the loss of Pitot's ships which had been seized in 1810. He also found that some members of the crew of the *Investigator* had not been properly paid off due to the fact that they had got back to England by various means and their commander had not been able to vouch for them. One of them was William Smith who had acted as his second servant until he had been released with other members of the crew of the *Cumberland.*

Thought was given to what the future might hold. Flinders did not want to go to sea again in the ordinary way, but he still pondered the idea that he might return to chart accurately the western coast of Australia, which he had had to pass speedily because of the need to get the *Investigator* back to Port Jackson before she became totally unseaworthy. However, he must have realised that with the enormous cost of the continuing Napoleonic wars, it was unlikely that an exploratory voyage could be financed. Writing to James Wiles, with whom he had corresponded since they served together in the *Providence*, he said he would probably buy a small house in the country and settle down to a quiet life, but should he sail again, the house would be a home for his wife, adding that he would go no more to sea unless it was upon discovery.

Flinders was never to know that Commander Philip Parker King, the grandson of the former Governor, was to make a further survey of the north eastern coast and to chart the western coast during expeditions he made between 1817 and 1822 and so complete the survey of the coastline of Australia. Writing in Sydney in 1853, King described Flinders as a distinguished officer to whom the colonists of Australasia and the commercial cities of Europe and America were under great obligations. He described how Flinders had executed a series of skilful surveys with less equipment than any navigator who had been engaged on similar duty in the previous fifty years and not only had his charts remained as sure guides to mariners, but they were mementoes of his courage, skill and perseverance.

Flinders heard a rumour that the governor of the Royal Naval College at Portsmouth might be retiring and asked if he might be considered as his successor, but was told the post was not likely to be vacant for some years. Other possibilities were explored, such as teaching in a nautical college, but until the book was finished no definite posts could be considered.

In March 1812 Flinders was asked to appear before the House of Commons Committee on Transportation together with John Hunter, the former Governor of New South Wales, and Henry Waterhouse, who had commanded H.M.S. *Reliance*. Questioned on what area he would particularly recommend for colonisation he suggested the Derwent River in Tasmania. He was also asked if he knew the north western coast of the island, to which he replied that he had discovered it.

All the time the work of writing up the account of the voyage had to go on. With his fluency in writing this in itself was not a burden, in spite of the absolute accuracy required in the navigational details, as he had the records in his journal made aboard the *Investigator*. It must be realised, however, that everything was written by hand, using a quill pen: the draft would have to be copied and checked and finally a fair copy made for the printers. Ann is recorded as sometimes helping with the checking. It was necessary to have these copies in case one was mislaid: the printer did manage to mislay one of the charts. It was the remaking of the charts ready to be engraved that took inordinate time and care.

As time went on social life lessened, and the journal records getting up at 6.30 or 7.0 each day to work before breakfast. He sat at his table again and worked through until dinner which was taken at 5.0 in the evening, unless he had to call on such people as Joseph Banks or John Barrow at the Admiralty, or the printer and the engraver. The journal sometimes records working until 10 o'clock at night "as usual". In the mornings and evenings of summer time this would not have been so difficult as in the candlelight of winter time.

There was some difference of opinion about the title of the book. New Holland was a name familiar to chart makers and both Arrowsmith, the engraver, and Banks had to be persuaded that Terra Australis was a more appropriate name for the whole land mass comprising New Holland, New South Wales and Van Diemen's Land. Banks would not accept the name Australia and this was a disappointment to Flinders as he thought it more pleasant to the ear. He did insist that the chart he had finalised when in Mauritius should remain "A General Chart of Terra Australis or Australia".

Flinders' health had been good since he returned home, except for the occasional times when he suffered from stones in the kidneys which he called his "gravelly complaint". By February 1814 he admitted that he had had this trouble rather often during the previous few months. A surgeon was consulted but with such medical treatment as was available at the time there was little that could be done. Gradually he found he could not sit at his table for more than twenty minutes at a time, before having to rest on a sofa, but with great determination he finished his writing and on the 26th and 27th May checked the last of the proof sheets. The book amounted to some 310,000 words and was divided into two volumes, which included appendices showing tables of magnetic variations and a contribution by Robert Brown, the naturalist, about the botany of Australia. There were also sixteen of Flinders' charts, five of William Westall's coastal sketches and ten of Ferdinand Bauer's botanical drawings, all of which were produced separately.

From the end of May his journal carefully records the various medicines he took and the names of visitors who called to see him whilst he lay on a sofa. Amongst them were William Westall, Robert Brown, John Fowler, the Franklins, Samuel Flinders and the Desbassayns, all of whom realised that he was in severe pain and unlikely to live.

In June young Anne had measles and her mother wrote to Isabella Tyler asking her to come down from Lincolnshire to help with nursing care and she was shocked at his appearance. In July the last sad entry in the journal reads: "Sunday 10th. Did not rise before two, being I think weaker than before".

He became semi-conscious and is said to have asked "Where are my papers?" The work to which he had given so much was published on 18th July 1814. Ann sent for a copy and placed it beside him, but he probably did not realise it and he died early in the morning of 19th July aged just 40 years.

14

The Widow's Mite

It has happened so often throughout history that the wives of men who went out across the world on great voyages of discovery or who lost their lives whilst serving their country were left in financial difficulties in their widowhood. Ann was one of them.

After the funeral service at St James' Church, Samuel Flinders, Willingham Franklin, George Nicol and "another gentleman" whose name is not recorded followed the coffin to the cemetery which was along the Hampstead road.

Deeply devoted to each other as they were it is not difficult to imagine Ann's grief, but she valiantly coped with the many problems with which she was now faced. As they had had to live on half-pay she would have known that she would have to live very modestly, but that her husband had some investments and that she would be entitled to a pension.

Flinders had made a new Will in 1812 and it would seem that he felt some responsibility towards members of his family. He left an annuity of £10 a year to his step-mother and gifts of £100 to his brother, Samuel, and to his sister Susanna Pearson, and a number of smaller gifts to other relatives. He also willed that £100 should be set aside to pay for memorial tablets in Donington church. This was an age when it was considered proper to put up such memorials and he may have felt that as the eldest son it was a duty he owed to his family. Nevertheless, it was a large sum to pay out and it was money that Ann felt should have been used to supplement the annuity of £55 a year she was to receive from his estate and the pension of £90 from the Navy to which she was entitled. Land had been bought in Mauritius as an investment, but there were complications about its sale and it was many years before Ann had any benefit from it.

When the Will was made Matthew was only thirty eight and seemed in normal health: immediate provision for his widow appeared unlikely. Immersed as he was in writing his "Voyage to Terra Australis", he had visualised taking another appointment giving him an income from which he would have been able to continue to add to the careful investments he had made until he was put on half pay. By the time his writing was nearly completed he was becoming ill, but in addition, it still being the Age of the Enlightenment, the fever of discovery had turned into a fever to share his knowledge and was made more acute because of the years of delay. When he realised he was dying he was possibly too ill to think coherently about his own affairs.

Inevitably, having only been able to accumulate a small amount of capital, Ann would have had only a limited income, but the amount he had willed to others meant that it was even more restricted. It is hard to believe, devoted as he was to her, that he realised the full implications of the dispositions he had made in his Will.

In December after her husband's death Ann wrote in a letter to Charles Hursthouse, with whom she had stayed in Lincolnshire in 1810, that "had my dear Captain F. seen his danger he would never have left me in such a situation". She went on to say that he was bent on concluding the writing up of his voyage without reverting to his own affairs, otherwise he would not have left so much to others and so would have provided better for her.

Flinders had been told that he would receive the profits from the book. Unfortunately the profit was to amount to only £190. The book sold for 12 guineas, a specialist and expensive book, so there was a limited sale and some copies ordered in Mauritius were destroyed in a fire there. The sad truth is that England was worn out by the Napoleonic wars and there was little interest left in hearing of discoveries of far flung places that had taken place over ten years ago. If it had not been for the long imprisonment in Mauritius it might have been different. As it was Joseph Banks was advising that the new lands should be regarded as a convenient place to send convicts and those who went out voluntarily to seek a new life now did so at their own peril.

James Cook had been murdered in dramatic circumstances at a time when interest in exploration was keen and his widow had been awarded a special pension of £200. It is possible that Flinders may have thought his widow would receive an equal amount. Efforts were made by Joseph Banks and William Wilberforce to get a similar pension for Ann, Flinders having completed the work which Cook had begun. When George IV had been Prince Regent he had shown no interest in the problem of Flinders living on half pay, nor would he have been likely to have any thought for the widow. When William IV succeeded his brother an approach was made to him. He said he saw no reason why Matthew Flinders' widow should not receive the same pension as the widow of James Cook, and he asked Lord Melbourne to look into it. However it was to no avail. In writing his "Life of Matthew Flinders" in 1914 Professor Ernest Scott mentioned that no official reward was granted by the British Government for the great services and discoveries of Flinders and commented that this stinginess was a depressing subject on which to reflect in a case of this kind.

Ann kept up a correspondence with Thomas Pitot who did his best to help with the sale of the property in Mauritius. It was two months after he died that she wrote to give "the mournful intelligence of the death of my dear husband". It is a long letter in which she said that she need not describe the measure of his worth, and goes on to say that for more than twenty years he was the idol of her heart and the centre of her earthly happiness, and although parted for nine years her affection for him never faltered. Ann was to take on the task of helping Pitot get compensation for the ships he had lost and she arranged for copies of *The Times* to be sent regularly, but had to ask him to pay for this.

Ann had always painted skilful and decorative flower pictures and this she continued to do, although finding paper expensive occasionally she used blank pages from the back of her husband's writings. Some of these paintings may be seen at Edward King House in Lincoln having been lent by the Flinders' family. Ann also wrote a memoir of his life ending that she hoped his name would stand equal in the annals of discovery with such men as Dampier, Bourgainville, Bligh and Pérouse or even "the immortal Cook".

For about a year Ann and her daughter continued to live in the house in King Street: Isabella remained with them, and they were joined by their mother. They were to move a number of times, living in Southampton, Bath, Reading and London again. Matthew's papers were all carefully packed and moved with them which has meant that today we have such a detailed record of his life. After Ann's death the family continued to care for the mass of letters and documents, but gradually distributed them to libraries in Australia and England.

It was not until 1851 that Matthew and Ann's daughter married William Petrie, a civil engineer, and, with Isabella, Ann moved to the house in Woolwich next door to the Petrie household. She died the following year and was buried at St Thomas' Church, Charlton.

In 1853 the governments of Victoria and New South Wales, learning about Ann's financial circumstances, offered her a pension of £100 a year from each government. Ann having died, it was agreed that the pension should devolve upon her daughter and she used the money for the education of her son who was born that year. It was a generous gesture on the part of two colonial governments. Inheriting his grandfather's zeal for discovery, although in a different field, he spent much time in Egypt and died in Jerusalem in 1942, having become the very distinguished archaeologist, Sir William Matthew Flinders Petrie.

15

Memorial

There are no houses left in England with which Matthew Flinders was associated. The house where he was born and the house in which he died have long since been pulled down, as has the house where he lived in Mauritius. As for his grave, when his daughter went to visit it some forty years after his death she found it had been swept away in a road widening scheme.

There is a memorial and a window in Donington Church; Partney Church has a tablet inside recording his marriage, and outside there is a stone erected by the Royal Geographical Society of Australasia. In St Botolph's church in Boston Flinders' name is included in the memorial to Lincolnshire men who sailed in the *Endeavour* and the *Investigator*. Australia has memorial stones at a number of places round the coast and there are statues in Melbourne, Adelaide and Sydney.

Ann Flinders deserves to be remembered for her enduring love of her husband in face of their long separation and the hardships she bore with courage.

Matthew Flinders should be remembered for his life of utter dedication to what his wife called "his darling discovery" which is encapsulated in "A Voyage to Terra Australis". His true memorial is in the great volume of his writing, his charts, his map of the continent he was the first to circumnavigate and above all in the name he gave it — Australia.

Coda

Samuel Flinders returned home with the China Fleet (merchant ships carrying tea to England). On the way they encountered the French Squadron commanded by Admiral de Linois, but due to the quick actions of both Samuel Flinders and Robert Fowler, de Linois drew away. Both officers were commended when they arrived home.

From the time Samuel joined Matthew aboard HMS Reliance at the age of twelve his elder brother felt he had a responsibility for him. It was not always an easy relationship, but Matthew recognised the considerable contribution that Samuel had made towards the work of the astronomical calculations when aboard the *Investigator*.

In 1820 Samuel married Mary Ann Bolton, a clergyman's daughter, at Nedging in Suffolk. They had three daughters and a son who was named Matthew. One of Samuel's grand-daughters, Cecilia, married William Petrie as his second wife. Samuel died in 1842 and is buried at Donington Church.

Robert Fowler was charged with the duty of bringing home and delivering to the Admiralty a quantity of the officers' journals and papers from the *Investigator* that had survived the shipwreck of the *Porpoise*. It was Fowler who had advised the Commodore of the China Fleet that sufficiently powerful guns should be carried and naval officers of experience should direct them if the ships were attacked. He was promoted to the rank of Commander in 1806 and later became an Admiral.

John Franklin also returned to England with the China

Fleet, and joining the *Bellepheron*, he took part in the Battle of Trafalgar. He was involved in naval actions against the United States in 1814. Between 1818 and 1827 he made voyages of exploration to the Arctic, following which he was appointed Governor of Tasmania. He lost his life in 1847 whilst making a further voyage to the Arctic.

Samuel Smith was another who came back with the China Fleet. On arrival he had the misfortune to encounter the Press Gang and was forced to remain in the Navy until 1815. "The Manchester Gazette" reported that he had died on the 29th January 1821, aged 50, and carried a short note about his sailing with Matthew Flinders and that he had kept a journal recording his experiences.

Charles De Caen, having been sent back to France after the surrender of Mauritius, returned to the Army and was appointed to a command in Spain. Later he served in the Netherlands and at Bordeaux, which had been occupied by the British. After the fall of Napoleon, De Caen was held prisoner for fifteen months before he retired to his country home where he died in 1832.

Note 1

Orders issued by Matthew Flinders as the *Investigator* sailed:

Sunday July 19, 1801

On getting to sea, I this afternoon issued the following order, directed to the boatswain, gunner, and carpenter of the ship. The length of time that the present voyage may be expected to require, making a particular care of the stores a matter of the first importance, it is my directions to Mr. Charles Douglas, boatswain, to Mr. Robert Colpits gunner, and to Mr. Russel Mart carpenter, of His Majesty's sloop under my command, that they do not issue any stores of any kind however small the quantity, to any officer or man whatever, without my permission; and if any officer sees the necessity of replacing any thing that may be deficient, or to apply stores to any use that may be wanted, he is requested to mention it to the Commander for his approbation, before he orders the warrant officer to issue; since it cannot be complied with in consequence of this order. It is, however, to be understood, that in cases of imminent danger, or immediate necessity, where timely application cannot be made to me, that the commanding officer be authorized to give such orders relative to the stores as he may judge necessary, and as if this order had not been given.

Mattw. Flinders

To the officers of the ship I also issued some instructions, which are as follow.

Directions to be observed by the officers of the watch.

1st. On relieving the deck, particularly in the night, he is to see that the lookout is attended to, that the ropes are properly belayed and coiled fair, and that the sails are properly trimmed; for he is not to permit a sail to remain set in a slovenly or improper manner because he found it so. The weather lifts, braces, and backstays are recommended to his constant attention, more especially when it blows fresh.

2. The watch is to be mustered at the first quarter hour of the watch; and if any are absent, the officer is himself to inquire into the cause, and to punish the absentees moderately, or to excuse their attendance as shall appear to him proper. In cases of repeated or material neglect, he is referred to the 2nd article of his instructions. The people are to be mustered at any other time or times in the watch if the officer suspects that any are absent.

3. One man at least, is to be kept looking out at night; and in particular cases by day also; and never to be taken off but upon some particular emergency, and to be replaced as soon as possible. The person looking out is to be relieved every hour or oftener, and frequently visited. The day look out is to be at the fore top-mast head, and when it is not constant, a man is to be sent up to look well round every two hours, as also before dark and at sunset daylight.

4. He is strictly to forbid any person from taking off the attention of the helmsman from the steerage of the ship.

5. It is expected, that from his own observation, he shall know the course which the ship has been steered for each hour, that he may be able to correct any inaccuracies that have been made in marking the log board; and he is to notice whether the mate of the watch applies to the quarter master or helmsman for an account of the ship's course, and if he does observe it,

he is to reprimand him for the inattention that makes an application to them necessary.

6.　He is constantly to inform the Commander of any material alteration in the wind or weather, and not to make any alteration of consequence in the quantity of sail without his knowledge, unless in cases of immediate necessity. With respect to alterations in the course, he is referred to the 4th article of his instructions.

7.　The officer of the watch is desired to put the initials of his name upon the log-board at the end of his watch; and is expected to answer for the correctness of what is there marked. If he suspects the accuracy of the copy in the log-book, he may examine it before it is brought in to me, which will be regularly done before one oclock.

8.　The height of the thermometer in the shade is to be marked at the end of each watch both by night and by day. At noon, a bucket of sea water is to be drawn and the thermometer immersed in it, and its height marked on the log board also. At daylight and at noon, the height of the marine barometer is to be marked in its column on the board.

9.　At the earliest opportunity every morning watch the topsail sheets are to be trimmed boused home, and all the sails hoisted up fair and properly and at seven bells, the hammocks to be piped up and the between decks swept out. It is expected that of the officer of the morning watch, that he use every exertion to have the sails, the upper and lower decks, the ropes and hammocks in a proper state for the people to go to breakfast at eight oclock. When circumstances will permit they are to be allowed an hour to breakfast.

10.　He is to take care that the boatswain and carpenter, or their mates, do examine the state of the rigging, the masts and yards, before the hammocks are piped up.

The captains of the tops and of the after guard are to accompany the boatswain or mate in his examination; and whatever is amiss is to be replaced, reported to the officer, and repaired as soon as possible.

11. The officer of the morning watch and his mates and midshipman are to attend to any duty that may be required from the watch below during the day. The lower deck is to be washed and aired or cleaned, in the best manner that the weather and the duty of the ship will permit; and the officer is to report to me when such cleaning is done, that I may inspect into it.

12. The hammocks are to be piped down at 6 pm and afterwards the ship pumped out, the decks swept, (and wetted when within the tropics) and the ropes coiled fair for performing any evolution during the night. These necessary duties are to be completed before 8 pm.

13. He is desired to be very particular in mentioning to the officer that relieves him, the exact state of the sails, and the orders that may have been left with him, and every other thing which it may be necessary for him to know.

An account of the ship's situation at noon each day, is expected from the commissioned officers of the ship; and it is wished that this situation may be found by astronomical observation as often as possible. Attention to this branch of science from the principal officers is of consequence in the present voyage, both from its utility, and as an example to the inferior officers.

As the Commander expects, that when an officer receives an order, he will never lose sight of it until not only the letter of it, but also the intention of the spirit of the order are fulfilled; so he requests, that the officers will never permit the petty officers or men, either to neglect any duty which they may have ordered, or to execute it any otherwise than completely and expeditiously. A due attention to these points is the very essence of discipline and good order and therefore the Commander begs to press it upon the consideration of the officers very particularly. From the masters mates and midshipmen of the ship much is expected.

1st. In relieving the watch, they are expected to show an example of alertness to the men. They are not to leave the deck without being relieved, or having the permission of the officer of the watch so to do who in that case is answerable for their duty; and this indulgence is not to be abused. They are to be attentive to the orders given by the officer, which they are not only to repeat, but to see them executed and when a particular duty is ordered, the mate or midshipman who is appointed to superintend is in most cases to report when it is executed. They are expected to give manual assistance when circumstances require it, and when a topsail is reefed, or any material duty going on in the top, the senior midshipman is to attend there. The duty of the mizzen top is solely to be done by the younger gentlemen, as far as their strength will enable them to do it. Upon all duties, the Commander expects to see them forward and active, and anxious to give every assistance in their power.

2. They are never to take off the attention of the helmsman by talking to him or otherwise.

3. A days work is expected from the masters mates, and from every midshipman who has any expectation of being rated as such. It is to contain the situation by log, the observed latitude as taken and worked by themselves, and the longitude by any astronomical observation that they may be master of. Such as are unacquainted, it behoves to apply themselves and those whose application entitles them to notice will be permitted to work in the cabin, and will have every assistance from the astronomer and Commander, to

make them perfect in this part of their profession. They will also be initiated into the manner of making marine surveys and constructing charts; by which means they may make themselves useful in the voyage, and lay a foundation for their own future promotion.

4. On the first day of every month, the mates and such midshipmen as expect to be rated, are desired to send in their journals to the Commander for his inspection; as also a complete watch bill, quarter bill, station bills for tacking and unmooring ship; and an order book in which the present orders are to be inserted, as also such as may be hereafter given out.

Mattw. Flinders.

Note 2

Matthew Flinders' full report given at Port Jackson is given below:

> Our stay in Port Jackson being now completed, it may be proper to make a short statement of the advantages we derived from being there, and of the observations made during our stay.
>
> The principal objects in view, in coming into this port, are briefly the following:
>
> 1. To refresh the ships company
>
> 2. To complete the provisions for a twelve months expedition round New Holland.
>
> 3. To make a thorough examination into the state of all the stores on board, and to have surveys upon them to enable the different officers to pass their annual accounts.
>
> 4. To complete the charts of the south coast of New Holland; and to get copies of them made and sent home to my Lords Commissioners of the Admiralty.
>
> 5. To ascertain the errors of the time-keepers in longitude and get fresh rates for them.
>
> 6. To make up the deficiencies in the ship's company, which the loss of the boat's crew near Uncertain Island had made considerable; and also to get another boat in lieu of that lost.
>
> 7. To set up the greenhouse for the reception of exotic plants; and
>
> 8. To consult with His Excellency the governor as to the best means of executing the remaining part of my

instructions for the examination of New Holland.

How far we fulfilled these objects will partly appear from the preceding journal but more concisely as follows:

1.   In refreshing the ship's company, we were obliged to trust more to their individual exertions than to any public purchases: the price of fresh meat being so very exorbitant. His Excellency once exchanged a day's fresh beef with us for salt pork and occasionally gave us a basket of vegetables.   Fish it was difficult to get in the winter season and our necessary duties did not permit us to send away men to fish without more certainty of success; a few were, however, occasionally purchased alongside.   In lieu of the pound of biscuit, 1¼ lbs of soft bread was issued to the people daily, without any additional expense. The officers and many of the ship's company, generally had vegetables at their tables, and sometimes poultry, but which was not obtained at a small expense.   On going to sea, I purchased sheep at £3 per head: pigs at 9d. per lb alive, geese at 10s. each and fowls at 3s. each.

2.   In completing our provisions for a further expedition, we were very fortunate.   I entered into a contract for 30,000 lbs of biscuit, 8000 lbs of flour and 156 bushels of wheat; but in the interim a twelve months provisions arrived for the ships from England, agreeably to my application to the Admiralty of July 18, 1801; upon which I prevailed upon the contractor to annul the part which related to flour and wheat; but I took the bread, for which 33s. per hundred pounds, was paid. In every other respect we completed up to a twelve month, except with spirits which had not arrived; and I left the remaining provisions in the public stores, under charge of the commissary, for our future use. From two American vessels which arrived, I purchased 1483 ¼ gallons of rum, at 6/6 per gallon; which, with what remained of our former stock, was equal to our

proportion of other provisions.

3.   The stores of every kind were well examined and surveys of the whole were taken and sent home. The two suits of sails which had been sent, required to be repaired, and the sailmakers were accordingly employed in that duty the greater part of our stay.

On considering the state of our sails and the service which we should have for them, I thought it necessary to write home for another suit and some other stores being likely to be wanted, a demand was sent as follows:

Boatswains Stores	Provisions for 90 men
One suit of sails complete	Beef and pork for 6 months
Two 13 ½ inch cables	Pease – Do
One 8 inch stream cable	Spirits – Do
Two 8 inch messengers	Lime juice – Do
One 5 inch hawser	Essence of malt
One 22 cwt. Bower anchor	Mustard in bottles – Do
Two barrels of tar	Essence of spruce – Do
40 gallons of black varnish	Molasses – Do
Sourkrout – Do	

Carpenters stores

Linseed oil – 50 gallons

I had purchased for the use of the people 978 lbs of tobacco, being able to buy it for as little as 6d per pound at that time; and our stock of that article being nearly expended, and a part damaged.

4.   This object of our putting into Port Jackson was completely fulfilled.

From the astronomical journal, the log, the bearing

book, and from the rough chart I constructed a series of charts of the whole south coast, and some larger scales of other particular parts.

Of these charts I had two copies made, by one of the young gentlemen on board; the one to be transmitted home to the admiralty, and the other to be left in the hands of the governor, and to be forwarded to England in case of the loss of the ship, lest the copy sent might fail. By a prior conveyance I transmitted to the Admiralty an account of the principal discoveries made upon the south coast, but the charts were not then ready. Mate of the ship *Hercules* was entered as an acting master, — three men were exchanged who were not fit for active service, and a marine invalided and sent home; and the places of these were all filled up, so that we sailed with a full complement of men. Some of those entered being convicts, His Excellency governor King, gave me an instrument relating to them, which is as follows:

By His Excellency Philip Gidley King, Esquire; Captain General and Governor in Chief in and over His Majestys Territory of New South Wales and its Dependencies, etc. etc. etc.

Whereas captain Matthew Flinders, Commander of His Majesty's sloop *Investigator* has requested permission to receive on board that ship the undermentioned convicts as seamen to make up the number he is deficient I do hereby grant Thomas Toney, Joseph Tuzo, Thomas Shirley, Francis Smith, Thomas Smith, Joseph Marlow, Thomas Martin, Richard Stephenson and Charles Brown permission to ship themselves on board His Majesty's sloop *Investigator*. And on the return of that ship to this port according to Captain Flinder's recommendation of them severally and individually, they will receive Conditional Emancipations or Absolute Pardons as that officer may request.